CORNERSTONES

THE BIBLE AND JEWISH IDEOLOGY

RABBI HAYYIM ANGEL

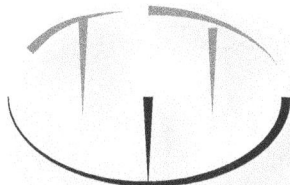

KODESH PRESS

Cornerstones: The Bible and Jewish Ideology
© Hayyim Angel, 2020

Paperback Edition
ISBN: 978-1-947857-43-8

Published & Distributed Exclusively by

Kodesh Press L.L.C.
New York, NY
www.kodeshpress.com
kodeshpress@gmail.com
sales@kodeshpress.com

SPONSORS

I thank my life-long friends for
their generous support of our ideas and ideals

Joshua Angel in memory of Rita Angel

The Cohenca Family
in honor of Rabbi Hayyim Angel

Marco Dilaurenti

Leonard and Chana Grunstein

Marjorie and John Lewin in
memory of Milton and Natalie Lewin

The Sephardic Publication Foundation and Its
Board Members: Isaac Ainetchi, Rabbi Marc D.
Angel, Simon Gerson, Andre Guenoun, Jane
Mushabac, Roberto Salama, and Ralph Sutton

When ten people sit together and study Torah, the
Divine Presence rests among them (Avot 3:6)

Dedicated by the Chaverim of the Beit Midrash of Teaneck who
are privileged to learn Torah with Rabbi Hayyim Angel.

Beth and Morris Apfelbaum

Rabbi Meier Brueckheimer

Esther and Myron Chaitovsky

Nechemia and Esther Crystal

Dr. Carl Feit

Tom and Marsha Friedman

Judy and Robert Friedman

Benjamin Gelbtuch

Dr. and Mrs. Andrew Geller

Ken Goldfarb

Len and Estee Goldsmith

Rabbi and Mrs. Norman Gorlyn

Leonard and Chana Grunstein

Marcia and David Jacobowitz

Lawrence J. Kaplan

Joseph and Sharon Penkower Kaplan

Dr. Chaim and Fay Feldman Kranzler

Marty and Rhonda Leibowitz

Tim and Ria Levart

Chaim Malks

Danny and Carol Metzger

Penina and Jay Orlinsky

Avrohm and Hetty Perl

Sherry and Bernie Perlowitz

Sharon and Naftali Ratzersdorfer

Arnold and Fran Rochwarger

Shuly and Albie Roth

Aaron and Jean Rothstein

Arlene and Michael Sand

Esther and Jackie Schlanger

Sylvia and Alan Schoffman

Alan Schoor

Sy Schulman

Bruno and Rebecca Segal

Tammy and Benjie Silverberg

Yisrael Silverman

Lois Blumenfeld and Dr. Norman Sohn

Rabbi Sam and Mrs. Lorraine Vogel

Neal and Barbara Yaros

Anonymous

TABLE OF CONTENTS

INTRODUCTION

The religious heart and soul of the Jewish people is the Hebrew Bible, often called by its Hebrew acronym Tanakh—based on its three sections: Torah, Neviim (Prophets), and Ketuvim (Holy Writings). All subsequent Jewish religious conversations filter through the prism of revealed prophecy. Concurrently, the teachings of the Oral Law and later rabbinic thought are indispensable guides to the true meaning of the sacred written texts and the lessons and laws emanating from them.

When it comes to ascertaining the eternal messages God and the prophets want to teach, commentators are locked in a perpetual state of debate. Many methodological considerations, assumptions, and perspectives lie behind any interpretation. As students, we are required to sort through the genuine text evidence and the assumptions of our commentators. The scholarly pursuit of Tanakh study as a cornerstone for building a robust religious life and a better society requires constant effort and attention. We must explore every avenue in the hopes of gaining increased clarity and meaning.

Concurrently, there is a sacred duty to move seamlessly from text analysis to the living experience with God and humanity that should emerge from learning Tanakh and the layers of rabbinic interpretation. This volume presents twelve articles that focus on that intersection between text and religious life.

The first six articles explore central religious and moral values from within biblical and rabbinic tradition: The Land of Israel, biblical and contemporary morality, superstition, responsibilities toward the resident alien, the prophet Amos' focus on ethical behavior as the cornerstone of a relationship with God, and two brazen biblical prayers and rabbinic responses. These articles are followed by a study of Sephardic biblical interpreters from the past 500 years and the need for educators to integrate their voices into the classroom setting. There are three articles on different aspects of biblical learning methodology: An investigation of the respective rules of *peshat* and *halakhah* and how they interact in Tanakh study, a non-dogmatic look at rabbinic Midrashim and how they may deepen our understanding of obscure biblical characters, and a more general piece on the interaction between religious and academic Bible study.

The book closes with two articles on religious ideology and the paths we should choose on the communal level to create an increased sense of Jewish unity. The article on dogma considers two fundamental approaches of the classical commentators and how each impacts on building community. The article on the thought of my father, Rabbi Marc D. Angel, outlines the central hallmarks of the Institute for Jewish Ideas and Ideals and their vital relevance in today's religious world.

Many of the articles in this volume are from publications and classes I have given for the Institute for Jewish Ideas and Ideals (jewishideas.org), where I serve as National Scholar. The Institute promotes an open discussion of the panoply of traditional opinions, past and present, with the goal of identifying the underlying worldview of sacred texts and stimulating religious development and building a stronger community. Through our writings and programs, we embrace the wholeness of the Jewish people, intellectual challenge and questioning, diversity of opinion, and other critical values.

◇◇◇

As always, thank you to my family for your love and encouragement: Mom and Dad; Ronda, Dan, Andrew, Jonathan, and Jeremy; Elana, Jamie, Jake, Max, Charlie, and Kara; Momma, Papap, Matt, Erin, Molly, and Emily; Nate, Kasey, Grace, and Jacob.

Thank you to my father and the Institute for Jewish Ideas and Ideals for promoting our unique religious vision and for giving me the opportunity to channel scholarship and teaching in promoting the core value issues that should shape our communal discourse. I thank our Board and our supporters and members for turning our vision into a reality through our extensive writings and programming.

Thank you to the sponsors of this book, whose generosity enables us to distribute copies to rabbis, educators, college students, and members of the Institute for Jewish Ideas and Ideals. I thank Joshua Angel, the Cohenca Family, Marco Dilaurenti, Leonard and Chana Grunstein, John and Majorie Lewin, and the Sephardic Publication Foundation and its board members.

Thank you to the participants in the Beit Midrash of Teaneck, with whom I have learned twice weekly over the past two years and who have built an exhilarating learning environment. It has been a singular privilege learning with you.

Thank you to Rabbi Alec Goldstein and Kodesh Press. Rabbi Goldstein has published several of my books and continues his tradition of careful editing and preparation of each volume.

Thank you to Professors Menachem Kellner and Joshua Berman, whose scholarship regularly enlightens me and who were truly generous with their time to write blurbs for this book.

Most importantly, I thank my wife Maxine, and our children Aviva, Dahlia, Mordechai, and Eliyahu. Through nearly eleven years of marriage, Maxine has been a magnificent life partner in every step of our miraculous journey together. Our children bring endless love, joy, pride, learning, and excitement into every day. There is no greater gift from God than having the opportunity to build a family together with you. I love you and look forward to writing many more chapters of our shared lives together with you.

Hayyim Angel
Rosh Hodesh Elul, 5780
August 21, 2020
Teaneck, New Jersey

The Land of Israel in the Bible

I
Israel in the Book of Genesis

The Land of Israel as Divine Gift, Heart of the Covenant, and Oath

The Torah does not begin with Abraham, nor does its story begin in the Land of Israel. Instead, the Torah opens by presenting a vision for all of humanity. In his introduction to the Book of Genesis, Rabbi Obadiah Sforno (1470-1550, Italy) observes that only after the three failures of Adam and Eve, the generation of the Flood, and the Tower of Babel, does God choose Abraham and his descendants to teach religious morality to the rest of the world. The Torah celebrates Abraham as the first person who was not only personally righteous, but who was also committed to teaching righteousness to his family and society:

> For I have singled him out, that he may instruct his children and his posterity to keep the way of the Lord by doing what is just and right, in order that the Lord may bring about for Abraham what He has promised him (Genesis 18:19).

Abraham's family is filtered through the rest of Genesis until it becomes clear that God selects the descendants of Jacob as the Chosen People.[1]

1

After Abraham arrives in Israel. God promises the land to Abraham and his descendants:

> The Lord appeared to Abram and said, "I will assign this land to your heirs." And he built an altar there to the Lord who had appeared to him (Genesis 12:7).

God reiterates this promise after Abraham's nephew Lot—his presumed heir until that point—moves to the wicked city of Sodom:

> And the Lord said to Abram, after Lot had parted from him, "Raise your eyes and look out from where you are, to the north and south, to the east and west, for I give all the land that you see to you and your offspring forever. I will make your offspring as the dust of the earth, so that if one can count the dust of the earth, then your offspring too can be counted. Up, walk about the land, through its length and its breadth, for I give it to you" (Genesis 13:14-17).

God again solemnly promises the land to Abraham and his descendants in the covenant between the halves:

> On that day the Lord made a covenant with Abram, saying, "To your offspring I assign this land, from the river of Egypt to the great river, the river Euphrates..." (Genesis 15:18).

In these three instances, God grants the Land of Israel to Abraham as a unilateral gift. In chapter 17, however, God introduces the idea of a mutual covenant, fulfilled through circumcision:

> I will maintain My covenant between Me and you, and your offspring to come, as an everlasting covenant throughout the ages, to be God to you and to your offspring to come. I assign

the land you sojourn in to you and your offspring to come, all the land of Canaan, as an everlasting holding. I will be their God (Genesis 17:7-8).

Professor Yehudah Elitzur observes that this passage expresses the notion that the Land of Israel is an essential component of the mutual covenant between God and Israel.[2] It also is critical to note that although God places covenantal obligations onto Abraham and his descendants, God already had made a unilateral gift of the Land to Abraham and his descendants prior to the mutual covenant.

In addition to God's promises to Abraham, God reaffirms the land covenant to Isaac and to Jacob:

[God said to Isaac:] I will assign all these lands to you and to your heirs, fulfilling the oath that I swore to your father Abraham (Genesis 26:3).

And the Lord was standing beside [Jacob] and He said, "I am the Lord, the God of your father Abraham and the God of Isaac: the ground on which you are lying I will assign to you and to your offspring. Your descendants shall be as the dust of the earth; you shall spread out to the west and to the east, to the north and to the south. All the families of the earth shall bless themselves by you and your descendants…" (Genesis 28:13-14).

And God said to [Jacob], "I am El Shaddai. Be fertile and increase; a nation, yea an assembly of nations, shall descend from you. Kings shall issue from your loins. The land that I assigned to Abraham and Isaac I assign to you; and to your offspring to come will I assign the land" (Genesis 35:11-12).

3

Before Jacob leaves home to go to Laban, Isaac also gives Jacob the blessing of Abraham, which includes possession of the land:

> May El Shaddai bless you, make you fertile and numerous, so that you become an assembly of peoples. May He grant the blessing of Abraham to you and your offspring, that you may possess the land where you are sojourning, which God assigned to Abraham (Genesis 28:3-4).

In addition to the divine gift of the land and the centrality of the land in the God-Israel covenant, God swears the land to Abraham following the Binding of Isaac:

> The angel of the Lord called to Abraham a second time from heaven, and said, "By Myself I swear, the Lord declares: Because you have done this and have not withheld your son, your favored one, I will bestow My blessing upon you and make your descendants as numerous as the stars of heaven and the sands on the seashore; and your descendants shall seize the gates of their foes" (Genesis 22:15-17).

After Abraham demonstrates his absolute commitment, God gives Abraham the greatest assurance. Professor Jon Levenson observes that there is no explanation in the Torah as to why God chose Abraham initially, but God's oath ratifies the covenant when Abraham passes this ultimate test. Abraham has vindicated God's choice.[3]

To summarize, God repeatedly promises the Land of Israel to the Patriarchs. In addition to the land serving as a divine gift, it also plays a central role in the mutual God-Israel covenant. God also makes an oath to give the land to Abraham and his descendants following the Binding of Isaac.

4

PURCHASING LAND IN ISRAEL

Although the Israelites conquer the land at the time of Joshua, several land purchases merit biblical attention. Abraham purchased the first family holding in Israel, the Cave of Machpelah in Hebron and its adjacent field in which he would bury Sarah:

> Then Abraham rose from beside his dead, and spoke to the Hittites, saying, "I am a resident alien among you; sell me a burial site among you, that I may remove my dead for burial…. Let [Ephron] sell me the cave of Machpelah that he owns, which is at the edge of his land. Let him sell it to me, at the full price, for a burial site in your midst" (Genesis 23:3-4, 9).

The Torah repeatedly refers to the sale of Machpelah, highlighting its significance. Abraham is buried there:

> His sons Isaac and Ishmael buried him in the cave of Machpelah, in the field of Ephron son of Zohar the Hittite, facing Mamre, the field that Abraham had bought from the Hittites; there Abraham was buried, and Sarah his wife (Genesis 25:9-10).

Jacob's dying words are about this transaction. When his sons bury him, the Torah again mentions the purchase:

> Then he instructed them, saying to them, "I am about to be gathered to my kin. Bury me with my fathers in the cave which is in the field of Ephron the Hittite, the cave which is in the field of Machpelah, facing Mamre, in the land of Canaan, the field that Abraham bought from Ephron the Hittite for a burial site—there Abraham and his wife Sarah were buried;

there Isaac and his wife Rebekah were buried; and there I buried Leah—the field and the cave in it, bought from the Hittites" (Genesis 49:29-32).

Thus his sons did for him as he had instructed them. His sons carried him to the land of Canaan, and buried him in the cave of the field of Machpelah, the field near Mamre, which Abraham had bought for a burial site from Ephron the Hittite (Genesis 50:12-13).

Later in Israel's history, David purchases the plot that will be used as the future Temple in Jerusalem. The acquisition was originally the threshing floor of Araunah (known as "Ornan" in the book of Chronicles). Like Abraham, David refuses to accept the area as a gift and insists on paying for it instead. He even uses the same term that Abraham did: *be-kesef malei*, "the full price":

But King David replied to Ornan, "No, I will buy them at the full price [*be-kesef malei*]. I cannot make a present to the Lord of what belongs to you, or sacrifice a burnt offering that has cost me nothing." So David paid Ornan for the site 600 shekels' worth of gold (I Chronicles 21:24-25).

The other Patriarchal land purchase occurs when Jacob purchases a plot of land near Shechem, establishing the first land holding for the living in the nation's history:

The parcel of land where he pitched his tent he purchased from the children of Hamor, Shechem's father, for a hundred *kesitahs* (Genesis 33:19).

When the people bury Joseph's bones in Shechem at the end of the Book of Joshua, narrative mentions the original purchase:

The bones of Joseph, which the Israelites had brought up from Egypt, were buried at Shechem, in the piece of ground which Jacob had bought for a hundred *kesitahs* from the children of Hamor, Shechem's father, and which had become a heritage of the Josephites (Joshua 24:32).

The Bible's ongoing interest in these purchases suggests a desire to guarantee Israel's ownership of these three areas. One Midrash (*Genesis Rabbah* 79:7) similarly concludes that nobody can claim that Israel stole Machpelah, Shechem, or Temple Mount.

JACOB AS HUMAN BEING AND COVENANTAL FIGURE

The traditional weekly Torah reading *Vayeitzei* is 148 verses long (Genesis 28:10-32:3). Rabbi Elhanan Samet[4] demonstrates that the entire passage is a single literary unit. Precisely at the center of this passage (Genesis 30:27-28), Laban invited Jacob to remain and work for wages. Surprisingly, Jacob agreed to stay for an indeterminate period of time, rather than returning to Israel. This moment is the turning point of the passage. In the first half of the *parashah*, Jacob built his family. In the second half, however, Jacob remained in Haran simply to earn money, something he could have done in Israel as well. Jacob fathered all his children in the first half of the *parashah*, and stopped abruptly in the second half. Moreover, in the second half of the *parashah*, Jacob's wealth aroused the jealousy of Laban's family, forcing Jacob and his family to flee.

To support his reading, Rabbi Samet quotes a Midrash that criticizes Jacob for lingering with Laban:

God said to him, "Return to the land of your ancestors and I will be with you—your father is waiting for you, your mother is waiting for you, I Myself am waiting for you!" Rabbi Ammi said in the name of Resh Lakish, "possessions acquired outside of Israel have no blessing associated with them; return to the land of your ancestors and I will be with you" (*Genesis Rabbah* 74:1).

Rabbi Samet observes that Jacob's failure was not in the realm of the ethical. Rather, it was in delaying the fulfillment of his covenantal role. There is no ethical problem with earning a living; however, Jacob was obligated to return to the land of his ancestors to fulfill the vow he had made years earlier in Bethel, and to honor his parents.

Although the Torah never explicitly links the slavery to any sin, several Midrashim and later commentators search for possible explanations. One recent opinion is that of Rabbi Yehudah Kiel, who submits that the Israelites should have left Egypt after the famine in Joseph's time; because they remained, they were enslaved.[5] Although the Torah does not clearly identify the non-return of the Israelites as sinful, it is curious that the family decided to remain in Egypt even after the famine had ended.

THE LAND OF ISRAEL AS CENTRAL
TO THE PEOPLE'S IDENTITY

At the end of his life, Jacob asks Joseph not to bury him in Egypt but rather in Israel. Joseph agrees. Surprisingly, Jacob then makes him swear:

And when the time approached for Israel to die, he summoned his son Joseph and said to him, "Do me this favor, place your hand under my thigh as a pledge of your steadfast loyalty: please do not bury me in Egypt. When I lie down with my fathers, take me up from Egypt and bury me in their burial place." He replied, "I will do as you have spoken." And he said, "Swear to me." And he swore to him. Then Israel bowed at the head of the bed (Genesis 47:29-31).

Rashi and Ramban explain that although Jacob trusted Joseph, he believed that Pharaoh never would allow Joseph to go unless he was bound by an oath. Joseph in fact invoked the oath when requesting permission of Pharaoh:

And when the wailing period was over, Joseph spoke to Pharaoh's court, saying, "Do me this favor, and lay this appeal before Pharaoh: 'My father made me swear, saying, "I am about to die. Be sure to bury me in the grave which I made ready for myself in the land of Canaan." Now, therefore, let me go up and bury my father; then I shall return.'" And Pharaoh said, "Go up and bury your father, as he made you promise on oath" (Genesis 50:4-6).

Rabbi Shlomo Riskin,[6] however, observes that when Joseph appeals to Pharaoh, he speaks to Pharaoh's court, that is, to Pharaoh's underlings. Joseph was second in command in all of Egypt, so why did he not personally ask Pharaoh?

Rabbi Riskin explains that this was a moment of truth for Joseph. He had been struggling with his identity ever since he had become second in command some 25 years earlier. Pharaoh gave him the Egyptian name Zaphenath-Paneah and married him to a daughter of the priest of On (Genesis 41:45). Joseph was a success, and Pharaoh made it clear that Joseph was an Egyptian.

Rabbi Riskin explains the names of Manasseh and Ephraim in light of Joseph's identity conflict. Manasseh represents Joseph's new

Egyptian identity: "God has made me forget completely [*nashani*] my hardship and my parental home." Ephraim, on the other hand, reminds Joseph that Egypt never will become his true home: "God has made me fertile [*hifrani*] in the land of my affliction" (Genesis 41:51–52).

Jacob understood that Joseph's identity would be tested severely by this request to be buried in Israel. Therefore, he made him swear. Joseph understood that by honoring his father's will, he would be making a public declaration that his family identity belongs to Israel and not to Egypt. He therefore was afraid to confront Pharaoh directly.

Joseph addresses his brothers on his deathbed: "Joseph made the sons of Israel swear, saying, 'When God has taken notice of you, you shall carry up my bones from here'" (Genesis 50:25). Joseph thereby confirms his Israelite identity by insisting that he will join his people in the future exodus.

SUMMARY

From the time Abraham arrived in Israel, God promises him and his descendants the land. This promise manifests as an outright unilateral gift, an essential part of a mutual covenant, and is ratified by divine oath after the Binding of Isaac. God repeats this promise to Isaac and Jacob.

Abraham's purchase of Machpelah in Hebron and Jacob's purchase of land in Shechem both receive significant attention, highlighting the permanence of these acquisitions prior to Joshua's later conquest of the land.

Jacob's extended sojourn at Laban's house to earn a living was morally justified, but it was unnecessary and therefore represented a delay in the fulfillment of his covenantal role. No blessing emerged from those additional six years away from Israel. Similarly, the family's decision to remain with Joseph in Egypt after the famine created the possibility of Israel's slavery under the following Pharaoh.

Jacob insisted on being buried in Israel, and Joseph needed to make a public statement that he too identified as an Israelite rather than as an Egyptian. On his deathbed, Joseph expressed his ultimate desire to be buried in Israel.

II

ISRAEL IN EXODUS THROUGH DEUTERONOMY

In Genesis, God makes an absolute, unbreakable covenant with Abraham. God promises that He will give the Land of Israel to Abraham's descendants (through Jacob's line) as an everlasting holding. The land is a gift under divine oath, and also is a central aspect of the God-Israel covenant:

> I assign the land you sojourn in to you and your offspring to come, all the land of Canaan, as an everlasting holding. I will be their God (Genesis 17:8).

In the rest of the Torah, however, God introduces a conditional aspect of this mutual covenant of the land. The blessings and curses in Leviticus 26, and several other passages, threaten exile if Israel sins:

I will lay your cities in ruin and make your sanctuaries desolate, and I will not savor your pleasing odors. I will make the land desolate, so that your enemies who settle in it shall be appalled by it. And you I will scatter among the nations, and I will unsheathe the sword against you. Your land shall become a desolation and your cities a ruin (Leviticus 26:31-33).

Take care not to be lured away to serve other gods and bow to them. For the Lord's anger will flare up against you, and He will shut up the skies so that there will be no rain and the ground will not yield its produce; and you will soon perish from the good land that the Lord is assigning to you (Deuteronomy 11:16-17).

One passage in Leviticus adds a poetic dimension. The Land of Israel is depicted as having a sensitive stomach, and it cannot tolerate grave sins. Sins cause the land to become ill and vomit out its inhabitants, whether Canaanite or Israelite:

Do not defile yourselves in any of those ways, for it is by such that the nations that I am casting out before you defiled themselves. Thus the land became defiled; and I called it to account for its iniquity, and the land spewed out its inhabitants. But you must keep My laws and My rules, and you must not do any of those abhorrent things, neither the citizen nor the stranger who resides among you; for all those abhorrent things were done by the people who were in the land before you, and the land became defiled. So let not the land spew you out for defiling it, as it spewed out the nation that came before you. All who do any of those abhorrent things—such persons shall be cut off from their people. You shall keep My charge not to engage in any of the abhorrent practices that were carried on before you, and you shall not defile yourselves through them: I the Lord am your God (Leviticus 18:24-30; cf. Leviticus 19:29; 20:22-25).

In addition to sexual crimes, the Torah also includes Molech worship (Leviticus 20:3; Deuteronomy 18:9-12), murder (Numbers 35:33-34), leaving a corpse of an executed person unburied (Deuteronomy 21:23), and violating the sanctity of marriage (Deuteronomy 24:1-4) as sins that pollute the land.[7] Later prophets present idol-worship as a sin that defiles the land. Thus, sin causes the land to become defiled, leading to the exile of its inhabitants.

The Torah presents antecedents for the ideas of exile and land defilement from the outset of creation. After Adam and Eve sin in Eden, God curses the earth and banishes Adam and Eve from Eden:

> To Adam He said, "Because you did as your wife said and ate of the tree about which I commanded you, 'You shall not eat of it,' cursed be the ground because of you; by toil shall you eat of it all the days of your life: Thorns and thistles shall it sprout for you. But your food shall be the grasses of the field".... So the Lord God banished him from the garden of Eden, to till the soil from which he was taken (Genesis 3:17-18, 23).

The Torah also expresses the poetic notion that the land cannot tolerate sin after Cain murders Abel. Having swallowed Abel's blood, the land no longer will produce for Cain, and Cain may not remain in his land:

> Then [God] said, "What have you done? Hark, your brother's blood cries out to Me from the ground! Therefore, you shall be more cursed than the ground, which opened its mouth to

receive your brother's blood from your hand. If you till the soil, it shall no longer yield its strength to you. You shall become a ceaseless wanderer on earth" (Genesis 4:10-12).

Throughout Tanakh, God reminds the Israelites that the land is not truly theirs, and they can be exiled if they fail to live up to the God-Israel covenant.

Joshua reiterates this threat shortly before his death, after the people already have possessed their land:

If you break the covenant that the Lord your God enjoined upon you, and go and serve other gods and bow down to them, then the Lord's anger will burn against you, and you shall quickly perish from the good land that He has given you (Joshua 23:16).

God also reminds Israel of the threat of exile for infidelity to their covenant, precisely at the ideal moment when Solomon dedicates the Temple:

[But] if you and your descendants turn away from Me and do not keep the commandments [and] the laws which I have set before you, and go and serve other gods and worship them, then I will sweep Israel off the land which I gave them; I will reject the House which I have consecrated to My name; and Israel shall become a proverb and a byword among all peoples (I Kings 9:6-7).

SABBATICAL AND JUBILEE YEARS

When Abraham needed a burial plot for Sarah, he faced a paradox. On the one hand, God had promised the land to him and his descendants for the future. On the other hand, he did not own any of that land and therefore was a resident alien (*ger ve-toshav*) among the Canaanites:

> I am a resident alien [*ger ve-toshav*] among you; sell me a burial site among you, that I may remove my dead for burial (Genesis 23:4).

Abraham wanted to gain a foothold in the land to bury Sarah as a landowner, rather than simply finding a spot on the roadside to bury her as a nomad.[8]

Even as the people of Israel are crossing the desert to possess their land, God insists that the land does not truly belong to them. Rather, it belongs to God and therefore the people must observe the Sabbatical and Jubilee years. They are resident aliens, just like Abraham:

> But the land must not be sold beyond reclaim, for the land is Mine; you are but strangers resident [*gerim ve-toshavim*] with Me (Leviticus 25:23).

The Torah also links the threat of exile to the violation of the laws of the Sabbatical and Jubilee years:

> I will make the land desolate, so that your enemies who settle in it shall be appalled by it. And you I will scatter among the nations, and I will unsheathe the sword against you. Your land shall become a desolation and your cities a ruin. Then shall the land make up for its Sabbath years throughout the time that it is desolate and you are in the land of your enemies; then shall the land rest and make up for its Sabbath years. Throughout the time that it is desolate, it shall observe the rest that it did not observe in your Sabbath years while you were dwelling upon it.... For the land shall be forsaken of them, making up

15

for its Sabbath years by being desolate of them, while they atone for their iniquity; for the abundant reason that they rejected My rules and spurned My laws (Leviticus 26:32-25, 43).

Non-observance of these laws demonstrates that the Israelites do not recognize that the land is God's, but instead consider the land to be their own.

At the very end of Tanakh, the Book of Chronicles reiterates this understanding when the people go into the Babylonian exile after the destruction of the Temple:

Those who survived the sword he exiled to Babylon, and they became his and his sons' servants till the rise of the Persian kingdom, in fulfillment of the word of the Lord spoken by Jeremiah, until the land paid back its Sabbaths; as long as it lay desolate it kept Sabbath, till seventy years were completed (II Chronicles 36:20-21).

Although Israel's continued presence in their land depends on their faithfulness to the covenant and their recognition that the land belongs to God, the land remains a permanent inheritance of the people of Israel. If they go into exile, they will always return to their land and no other nation will possess the land:

I assign the land you sojourn in to you and your offspring to come, all the land of Canaan, as an everlasting holding. I will be their God (Genesis 17:8).

The Book of Deuteronomy similarly reiterates the divine gift of the land to the people of Israel.[9] The Torah also restates God's oath guaranteeing this gift.[10] Specifically at times of great sin and crisis, the prophets invoke God's oath and eternal covenant with Israel.

These include the Golden Calf (Exodus 32:13-14) and the destruction of the Temple (Jeremiah 7:3-7; 33:25-26).

THE THREAT OF PROSPERITY AND
THE NEED TO BE GRATEFUL TO GOD

In addition to the Torah's concern that the people of Israel never consider the land to be absolutely theirs, the Torah repeatedly praises the beauty and fertility of the land and warns against losing sight of the fact that all blessings come from God.

During Moses' initiation prophecy at the burning bush, God praises Israel:

> "I am," He said, "the God of your father, the God of Abraham, the God of Isaac, and the God of Jacob." And Moses hid his face, for he was afraid to look at God. And the Lord continued, "I have marked well the plight of My people in Egypt and have heeded their outcry because of their taskmasters; yes, I am mindful of their sufferings. I have come down to rescue them from the Egyptians and to bring them out of that land to a good and spacious land, a land flowing with milk and honey, the region of the Canaanites, the Hittites, the Amorites, the Perizzites, the Hivites, and the Jebusites..." (Exodus 3:6-8).

This is the first of some twenty biblical references to Israel as the land of milk and honey.

In Deuteronomy, Moses repeatedly warns against the hazard of prosperity. If the people forget that all is from God and they become ungrateful, they will soon lapse into unfaithfulness:

> For the Lord your God is bringing you into a good land, a land with streams and springs and fountains issuing from

plain and hill; a land of wheat and barley, of vines, figs, and pomegranates, a land of olive trees and honey; a land where you may eat food without limit, where you will lack nothing; a land whose rocks are iron and from whose hills you can mine copper. When you have eaten your fill, give thanks to the Lord your God for the good land which He has given you. Take care lest you forget the Lord your God and fail to keep His commandments, His rules, and His laws, which I enjoin upon you today… and you say to yourselves, "My own power and the might of my own hand have won this wealth for me." Remember that it is the Lord your God who gives you the power to get wealth, in fulfillment of the covenant that He made on oath with your fathers, as is still the case (Deuteronomy 8:7-18).

The Talmud derives the commandment for the Grace After Meals from 8:10, "when you have eaten your fill, give thanks to the Lord your God for the good land which He has given you." The passage describes divine blessing, rather than using the typical language of commandment. However, Rabbi Joseph Soloveitchik observed that this verse must be read as a commandment. The continuation of the passage warns against what occurs when people do not bless God for their produce—they will forget God. Therefore, 8:10 must be a commandment of what Israelites must do to avoid this hazard, rather than a prediction of what they will do.[11]

ISRAEL'S DEPENDENCE ON RAINFALL AS A RELIGIOUS VALUE

The beautiful land depends on rainfall, requiring constant providential attention:

For the land that you are about to enter and possess is not like the land of Egypt from which you have come. There the grain you sowed had to be watered by your own labors, like a vegetable garden; but the land you are about to cross into and possess, a land of hills and valleys, soaks up its water from the rains of heaven. It is a land which the Lord your God looks after, on which the Lord your God always keeps His eye, from year's beginning to year's end (Deuteronomy 11:10-12).

Because of its consistent agricultural cycle, Egypt became a refuge during famines. The Torah likens Egypt to the Garden of Eden. Lot also moved to the wicked city of Sodom because it resembled Egypt and Eden in that the Jordan River watered the area and guaranteed fertility:

Lot looked about him and saw how well watered was the whole plain of the Jordan, all of it—this was before the Lord had destroyed Sodom and Gomorrah—all the way to Zoar, like the garden of the Lord, like the land of Egypt (Genesis 13:10).

God gave Israel a fertile land, but it is not consistently fertile as Egypt or Sodom. The latter are much easier places to obtain predictable prosperity. The consistent rising of the Nile and Jordan Rivers led to a state wherein people felt a sense of security and entitlement. There were no consequences to their sinful behavior, and both developed wicked cultures. Israel's dependence on rainfall, in contrast, fostered a culture of constant attention to relationship-building with a personal God.

Ramban (on Deuteronomy 11:11-12) similarly explains that all people depend on God, but a sick person feels that sense of dependence much more than a healthy person. Egypt is like a healthy person, and Israel is like a sick person. Since Israel depends on rain, the people must constantly remain conscious of their dependence on God.

PROFESSORS URIEL SIMON AND MOSHE GREENBERG

Professors Uriel Simon and Moshe Greenberg contribute additional dimensions of understanding to the religious significance of the Land of Israel in the Torah. Professor Simon[12] observes that Abraham's bond with the land is not natural, since he was not born there. Although God promises the land to Abraham and his descendants, Abraham must wait some 400 years for the fulfillment of this promise (Genesis 15:13-16). There is further uncertainty regarding the fulfillment of the divine promise because of the delay in Abraham's fathering an heir who would perpetuate the covenant.

Israel's connection to the land is not a natural bond; it is a connection of covenantal destiny. When a nation has a natural bond to its land, there is no constant threat of exile looming over the people. In contrast, when a nation has a covenantal relationship of destiny, this means that their rights to their land are based on a divine promise and are conditional on faithfulness to God.

A nation with a natural bond to its land loses that connection when it is exiled, and that nation ceases to exist. In contrast, a nation of destiny can temporarily lose its land, but retains an eternal bond to its land even when it goes into exile. Natural possession of one's land feels safe, but it deadens the heart of the nation since the people take their land for granted. Possession of land through destiny forces a nation to have constant attentiveness to God. Thus, the people of Israel never could take their land for granted, but also could retain their identity through their exile and long for a return to their land.

Professor Moshe Greenberg[13] explains that the Torah was given in the desert and its narrative ends with the people still in the desert. While many of the Torah's laws are applicable only in Israel, the basis for the God-Israel covenant is the exodus and revelation at

Sinai. If Israel is faithful to the Torah covenant, they will live safely in their land forever. If Israel is unfaithful, they can be exiled from land. Since the Torah transcends the Land of Israel, it remains fully binding outside of the land.

SUMMARY

The Torah makes the conditional aspect of the covenant explicit, threatening exile for certain grave sins. One passage in Leviticus adds the poetic dimension of the land becoming ill from sin, leading it to spew out its inhabitants. There are no purification rituals for the land, and only exile can allow the land to recover from its defilement.

The Sabbatical and Jubilee years convey the message that the land belongs to God and not to Israel. Non-fulfillment of these laws leads to exile, since Israel makes the false assumption that the land belongs to them. Even with exile, the land remains an eternal possession of the people of Israel and they will return to their land.

In addition to Israel's need to recognize that God owns the land, they also must be eternally grateful to God for the bountiful land and its produce. Proper gratitude lies at the heart of faithfulness to God, whereas ingratitude leads to unfaithfulness.

The Land of Israel's dependence on rainfall similarly creates a state of constant God-consciousness. Unlike Egypt and Sodom, which had the consistent rising of the Nile and Jordan Rivers, Israel felt their dependence on God at every moment.

Professor Uriel Simon develops the idea of the people of Israel's connection of destiny to their land. God's promises to Abraham are delayed—and are contingent on—Israel's faithfulness to the covenant. On the other hand, Israel's bond to its land cannot be severed by an exile, unlike nations that have a natural bond to their lands. The people of Israel always will return to their land.

Professor Moshe Greenberg highlights the fact that the Torah begins and ends outside of the Land of Israel to stress that it is an eternal covenant that transcends all land borders and applies wherever the people of Israel live. Israel is the place of ultimate fulfillment of the God-Israel relationship, but Israel has a covenantal relationship with God through the Torah everywhere.

III

ISRAEL IN THE PROPHETIC BOOKS

THE BOOK OF JOSHUA

There is no biblical holiday to celebrate Israel's entry to its land or Joshua's conquest of the land. Joshua even uses the Torah's language of a "proto-Seder" to commemorate the miraculous crossing of the Jordan River:

> This shall serve as a symbol among you: in time to come, when your children ask, "What is the meaning of these stones for you?" you shall tell them, "The waters of the Jordan were cut off because of the Ark of the Lord's Covenant; when it passed through the Jordan, the waters of the Jordan were cut off." And so these stones shall serve the people of Israel as a memorial for all time (Joshua 4:6-7).

> He charged the Israelites as follows: "In time to come, when your children ask their fathers, 'What is the meaning of those stones?' tell your children: 'Here the Israelites crossed the Jordan on dry land.' For the Lord your God dried up the waters of the Jordan before you until you crossed, just as the

Lord your God did to the Sea of Reeds, which He dried up before us until we crossed. Thus all the peoples of the earth shall know how mighty is the hand of the Lord, and you shall fear the Lord your God always" (Joshua 4:21-24).

Israel's memory is codified through the Torah's holidays to perpetuate the foundational experiences of the exodus, the revelation at Sinai, and the sojourn through the wilderness. Although the Land of Israel is a central aspect of the God-Israel relationship, the Torah applies everywhere, and not just in Israel.

Soon after crossing the Jordan River, Joshua fulfills the commandment to write the Torah on stones and to conduct a ceremony to accept the God-Israel covenant near Shechem at Mount Gerizim and Ebal (see Deuteronomy 11:26-32; 27:1-26):

At that time Joshua built an altar to the Lord, the God of Israel, on Mount Ebal, as Moses, the servant of the Lord, had commanded the Israelites—as is written in the Book of the Teaching of Moses.... And there, on the stones, he inscribed a copy of the Teaching that Moses had written for the Israelites. All Israel—stranger and citizen alike—with their elders, officials, and magistrates, stood on either side of the Ark, facing the levitical priests who carried the Ark of the Lord's Covenant. Half of them faced Mount Gerizim and half of them faced Mount Ebal, as Moses the servant of the Lord had commanded them of old, in order to bless the people of Israel. After that, he read all the words of the Teaching, the blessing and the curse, just as is written in the Book of the Teaching. There was not a word of all that Moses had commanded that Joshua failed to read in the presence of the entire assembly of Israel, including the women and children and the strangers who accompanied them (Joshua 8:30-35).

Writing the Torah on these stones, coupled with the recital of the blessings and curses of the Torah to the entire nation, establishes the Torah as the national charter for the people of Israel in their land. The Torah lies at the heart of the covenant at the gateway to the land.

The Talmud (*Sotah* 35b) suggests that the people wrote the Torah in all seventy languages of the nations of the world. Of course, this is not the plain sense of the text. Nevertheless, the Talmud stresses that, in addition to the Torah's centrality to the people of Israel, it also has a vision for all of humanity. Israel is to become a model nation whose religious morality inspires all people to recognize God's wisdom and justice exemplified by Israel's excellent conduct through the laws of the Torah:

> See, I have imparted to you laws and rules, as the Lord my God has commanded me, for you to abide by in the land that you are about to enter and occupy. Observe them faithfully, for that will be proof of your wisdom and discernment to other peoples, who on hearing of all these laws will say, "Surely, that great nation is a wise and discerning people." For what great nation is there that has a god so close at hand as is the Lord our God whenever we call upon Him? Or what great nation has laws and rules as perfect as all this Teaching that I set before you this day? (Deuteronomy 4:5-8).

In addition to the Torah's concern that Israel inspire and influence the nations of the world, the aforementioned passage in Joshua twice stresses that present at the ceremony were stranger and citizen alike (Joshua 8:33, 35). Already at the dawn of the nation of Israel's presence in their covenantal land, some non-Israelites joined them in accepting the Torah. The talmudic notion of the Torah being translated into seventy languages, then, is conceptually related to the biblical text.

THE TEMPLE IN JERUSALEM

David establishes Jerusalem as the political capital of Israel by moving there and building his palace (II Samuel chapter 5). He then establishes Jerusalem as God's capital by moving the Ark there (II Samuel chapter 6). God does not permit David to build the actual Temple, but assures him that his son will rule and build the Temple (II Samuel 7). Solomon goes on to build the Temple and a palace for himself near it (I Kings 6-7).

Ramban (on Exodus 25:2) explains that the Tabernacle (and the Temple) create a perpetual re-enactment of the Revelation at Sinai. Both Sinai and the Tabernacle had a tripartite division of holiness: (1) The mountain's summit is analogous to the Temple's Holy of Holies, accessible only to Moses or the High Priest. (2) The middle of the mountain is analogous to the Temple's Holy section, accessible only to the elders or the priests. (3) The base of the mountain is analogous to the Temple courtyard, where all people could gather to experience God's revelation.

In addition to Ramban's association of the Tabernacle-Temple with the Revelation at Sinai, several Midrashim ascertain connections between the Temple and the Garden of Eden. Ideally, Adam and Eve were supposed to follow God's commands and remain in the Garden. Instead, they sinned and were expelled, and God guarded the Tree of Life with Cherubim:

> [God] drove the man out, and stationed east of the garden of
> Eden the cherubim and the fiery ever-turning sword, to guard
> the way to the tree of life (Genesis 3:24).

In the time of Moses, the Torah replaced the Tree of Life with the Ark of the Covenant. Cherubim were placed above it, to guard it. The Tabernacle is the only other reference to Cherubim in the

25

Torah, and the Book of Proverbs refers to Torah and Wisdom as a Tree of Life: "She is a tree of life for those who grasp her" (Proverbs 3:18) (*Midrash ha-Gadol*, Genesis 3:24). Thus, the Tabernacle and Temple become a manifestation of the perfection in the Garden of Eden, where all humanity can live in harmony and serve God.

In addition to the Temple serving as the heart of the God-Israel relationship, Solomon also recognized the universalistic dimension of the Temple. In his prayer at the dedication of the Temple, Solomon stressed that all God-fearing people always are welcome. He expresses a longing for all humanity to recognize God:

> Or if a foreigner who is not of Your people Israel comes from a distant land for the sake of Your name—for they shall hear about Your great name and Your mighty hand and Your outstretched arm—when he comes to pray toward this House, oh, hear in Your heavenly abode and grant all that the foreigner asks You for. Thus all the peoples of the earth will know Your name and revere You, as does Your people Israel; and they will recognize that Your name is attached to this House that I have built…. And may these words of mine, which I have offered in supplication before the Lord, be close to the Lord our God day and night, that He may provide for His servant and for His people Israel, according to each day's needs—to the end that all the peoples of the earth may know that the Lord alone is God, there is no other (I Kings 8:41-43, 59-60).

The worldview underlying Solomon's prayer becomes a central feature of later prophetic visions, where the Temple serves as the religious center for both Israel and a God-fearing humanity.

The narratives in I Kings chapters 3-10 present Solomon's reign as the ideal period in Israel's history. Solomon is a wise king who judges the people fairly and is a prophet. The nation is religious and unified. There is peace and prosperity. God's Presence is manifest in the Temple. The nations of the world flood to Jerusalem to see the Temple and to admire Solomon's wisdom. Later prophets use this imagery to depict the ideal messianic age. The only element they add to their visions is that Israel's exiles will return to their land. During Solomon's reign, the Israelites still lived in their land and were not yet in exile.

THE DESTRUCTION OF THE TEMPLE AND EXILE

At the ideal moment in Israel's history, when Solomon dedicated the Temple, God warns that Israel can remain in this pristine state eternally only if they remain faithful to the Torah. If they violate the God-Israel covenant, they will lose the Temple and forfeit their right to remain in the land:

> [But] if you and your descendants turn away from Me and do not keep the commandments [and] the laws which I have set before you, and go and serve other gods and worship them, then I will sweep Israel off the land which I gave them; I will reject the House which I have consecrated to My name; and Israel shall become a proverb and a byword among all peoples (I Kings 9:6-7).

Tragically, King Solomon opened the door to idolatry toward the end of his life (I Kings 11), leading to the division of the monarchy. Sustained idolatry through much of the remainder of the period led to the eventual exile of the Northern Kingdom by the Assyrians, and ultimately the destruction of the Temple and exile by the Babylonians.

Living at the time of the destruction, the prophet Jeremiah understood that God's very creation was coming undone and returning to its primeval chaotic state:

> I look at the earth, it is unformed and void [*tohu va-vohu*]; at the skies, and their light is gone (Jeremiah 4:23).

This reference harks back to the second verse of the Torah, before God created order:

> The earth was unformed and void [*tohu va-vohu*], with darkness over the surface of the deep and a wind from God sweeping over the water (Genesis 1:2).

The destruction of the Temple ends the vision of its serving as a new Garden of Eden. The people of Israel are exiled to Babylonia and to Egypt (see II Kings 25), reversing Abraham's journey from the area of Babylonia as well as the exodus from Egypt in the time of Moses.

The Temple and Solomon's palace are destroyed together, as God's kingdom and Israel's kingdom fall to Babylonia:

> He burned the House of the Lord, the king's palace, and all the houses of Jerusalem; he burned down the house of every notable person (II Kings 25:9).

The destruction of the Temple and the exile sound like they are absolute, and most surviving Jews believed that God had abandoned them. The end of the Book of Lamentations poignantly reflects this dark despair of the people:

> But You, O Lord, are enthroned forever, Your throne endures through the ages. Why have You forgotten us utterly, forsaken

us for all time? Take us back, O Lord, to Yourself, and let us come back; renew our days as of old! For truly, You have rejected us, bitterly raged against us (Lamentations 5:19-22).

PROPHETIC VISIONS OF HOPE

Confronting the people's feelings of rejection, the prophets envisioned a time beyond the current reality and offered much-needed hope to the despairing people. In Isaiah 50, the prophet invokes the notion that the exile should be likened to a separation, but not a divorce:

Thus said the Lord: Where is the bill of divorce of your mother whom I dismissed? And which of My creditors was it to whom I sold you off? You were only sold off for your sins, and your mother dismissed for your crimes (Isaiah 50:1).

Alternatively, Jeremiah posited an even more extreme position that the exile was a divorce, but God still was prepared to remarry Israel if the people were to abandon their idolatry:

[The word of the Lord came to me] as follows: If a man divorces his wife, and she leaves him and marries another man, can he ever go back to her? Would not such a land be defiled? Now you have whored with many lovers: can you return to Me?—says the Lord (Jeremiah 3:1).

Regardless, the reality was the same: The God-Israel relationship is eternal. Either there never was a divorce, or there was a divorce with an ongoing invitation to return.

In his celebrated prophecy of the Dry Bones, Ezekiel depicts the people as feeling dead. God, however, will miraculously restore them to their vitality and to their land:

And He said to me, "O mortal, these bones are the whole House of Israel. They say, 'Our bones are dried up, our hope is gone [*avedah tikvatenu*]; we are doomed.' Prophesy, therefore, and say to them: Thus said the Lord God: I am going to open your graves and lift you out of the graves, O My people, and bring you to the land of Israel..." (Ezekiel 37:11-12).

This vision was intended as a parable to Israel. Like dead bones, Israel felt hopeless. God promised that He would restore life to the nation and bring them back to their land.[14]

In Isaiah 51, the prophet invokes God's eternal covenant with the Patriarchs, prophesying the nation's return to Israel and the restoration of the state of being like the Garden of Eden:

Listen to Me, you who pursue justice, you who seek the Lord: Look to the rock you were hewn from, to the quarry you were dug from. Look back to Abraham your father and to Sarah who brought you forth. For he was only one when I called him, but I blessed him and made him many. Truly the Lord has comforted Zion, comforted all her ruins; He has made her wilderness like Eden, her desert like the Garden of the Lord. Gladness and joy shall abide there, thanksgiving and the sound of music (Isaiah 51:1-3).

Ezekiel adds a further dimension: God must redeem the people to their land because their remaining in exile desecrates God's Name:

Say to the House of Israel: Thus said the Lord God: Not for your sake will I act, O House of Israel, but for My holy name, which you have caused to be profaned among the nations to which you have come. I will sanctify My great

30

name which has been profaned among the nations—among whom you have caused it to be profaned. And the nations shall know that I am the Lord—declares the Lord God— when I manifest My holiness before their eyes through you. I will take you from among the nations and gather you from all the countries, and I will bring you back to your own land (Ezekiel 36:22-24).

Although exile is a punishment for sin and it desecrates God's Name, it was to be the reality for the next two generations. Prior to the destruction of the Temple, Jeremiah corresponded with the community already exiled to Babylonia in 597 BCE with King Jehoiachin, instructing them to build a Jewish life while they waited for the restoration to their land. That restoration would come some seventy years after the rise of the Babylonian Empire:

Thus said the Lord of Hosts, the God of Israel, to the whole community which I exiled from Jerusalem to Babylon: Build houses and live in them, plant gardens and eat their fruit. Take wives and beget sons and daughters; and take wives for your sons, and give your daughters to husbands, that they may bear sons and daughters. Multiply there, do not decrease. And seek the welfare of the city to which I have exiled you and pray to the Lord in its behalf; for in its prosperity you shall prosper.... For thus said the Lord: When Babylon's seventy years are over, I will take note of you, and I will fulfill to you My promise of favor—to bring you back to this place (Jeremiah 29:4-10).

The Jews were to retain their identity while living in the Diaspora, but they always knew that they would return home to Israel.

THE AGRICULTURAL PRODUCTIVITY OF THE LAND OF ISRAEL

Israel's agricultural bounty is a recurring theme in later prophecies of restoration. For example, the Book of Amos concludes with a prophecy of restoration wherein God will restore Israel's beautiful produce, and implant the people Israel in their land:

> A time is coming—declares the Lord —When the plowman shall meet the reaper, and the treader of grapes him who holds the [bag of] seed; when the mountains shall drip wine and all the hills shall wave [with grain]. I will restore My people Israel. They shall rebuild ruined cities and inhabit them; they shall plant vineyards and drink their wine; they shall till gardens and eat their fruits. And I will plant them upon their soil, nevermore to be uprooted from the soil I have given them—said the Lord your God (Amos 9:13-15).

Rabbi Abba suggests that agricultural restoration is the surest sign of Israel's redemption:

> Rabbi Abba also said: There can be no more manifest [sign of] redemption than this: namely, what is said, "But you, O mountains of Israel, you shall shoot forth your branches, and yield your fruit to My people of Israel, for they are at hand to come" (Ezekiel 36:8, *Sanhedrin* 98a).

Israel's mission is to serve as a kingdom of priests and a holy nation (Exodus 19:6), the religious capital of the world that teaches humanity to return to the ideal state of the Garden of Eden:

> In the days to come, the Mount of the Lord's House shall stand firm above the mountains and tower above the hills; and all the

nations shall gaze on it with joy. And the many peoples shall go and say: "Come, let us go up to the Mount of the Lord, to the House of the God of Jacob; that He may instruct us in His ways, and that we may walk in His paths." For instruction shall come forth from Zion, the word of the Lord from Jerusalem. Thus He will judge among the nations and arbitrate for the many peoples, and they shall beat their swords into plowshares and their spears into pruning hooks: Nation shall not take up sword against nation; they shall never again know war (Isaiah 2:2-4).

The wolf shall dwell with the lamb, the leopard lie down with the kid; the calf, the beast of prey, and the fatling together, with a little boy to herd them. The cow and the bear shall graze, their young shall lie down together; and the lion, like the ox, shall eat straw. A babe shall play over a viper's hole, and an infant pass his hand over an adder's den. In all of My sacred mount nothing evil or vile shall be done; for the land shall be filled with devotion to the Lord as water covers the sea (Isaiah 11:6-9).

THE HOLINESS OF THE LAND OF
ISRAEL AND THE IMPURITY OF OTHER LANDS

The sanctity of the Land of Israel is not some metaphysical quality inherent in the land. Rather, sanctity derives from a covenantal relationship with God. Israel is called "the Holy Land" only once in all of Tanakh (Zechariah 2:16), and it was occupied by Canaanites before Israel arrived. The Talmud argues that human efforts by Joshua (via conquest) and later by Ezra (via settlement) were required to sanctify the land:

Many cities were conquered by those who came up from Egypt, which were not conquered by those who came up from Babylon; since the first consecration held [only] for the time, but did not hold for the future [permanently] (*Hagigah* 3b; cf. *Yevamot* 16a, *Makkot* 19a, *Hullin* 7a).

Rambam adopts this ruling as practical law (*Hilkhot Bet ha-Behirah* 6:16).

Conversely, lands other than Israel are impure, since Israelites cannot live a complete religious life outside of Israel. The Israelites living west of the Jordan River beckon the east bank tribes, who live in unclean land, to consider living with them:

If it is because the land of your holding is unclean, cross over into the land of the Lord's own holding, where the Tabernacle of the Lord abides, and acquire holdings among us. But do not rebel against the Lord, and do not rebel against us by building for yourselves an altar other than the altar of the Lord our God (Joshua 22:19).

Amos similarly tells the wicked priest Amaziah that he will die on unclean soil, that is, in exile (Amos 7:17). The exiles to Babylonia feel as though they cannot even praise God on foreign soil:

How can we sing a song of the Lord on alien soil? (Psalm 137:4).

The most dramatic expression of lands outside of Israel being unclean is when David must flee from King Saul:

For they have driven me out today, so that I cannot have a share in the Lord's possession, but am told, "Go and worship other gods" (I Samuel 26:19).

David's makes it appear that by leaving the Land of Israel, he must worship other gods! Although the verse should not to be taken literally, the Talmud understands that there is something fundamentally lacking in the God-Israel relationship when one lives outside of Israel:

> One should always live in the Land of Israel, even in a town most of whose inhabitants are idolaters, but let no one live outside the Land, even in a town most of whose inhabitants are Israelites; for whoever lives in the Land of Israel may be considered to have a God, but whoever lives outside the Land may be regarded as one who has no God. For it is said in Scripture, "To give you the Land of Canaan, to be your God" (Leviticus 25:38). Has he, then, who does not live in the Land, no God? But [this is what the text intended] to tell you, that whoever lives outside the Land may be regarded as one who worships idols. Similarly, it was said in Scripture in [the story of] David, "For they have driven me out this day that I should not cleave to the inheritance of the Lord, saying: Go, serve other gods" (I Samuel 26:19). Now, whoever said to David, "Serve other gods"? But [the text intended] to tell you that whoever lives outside the Land may be regarded as one who worships idols (Ketuvot 110b).[15]

A similar idea is found in Deuteronomy, where idolatry is a consequence of going into exile:

> The Lord will scatter you among the peoples, and only a scant few of you shall be left among the nations to which the Lord will drive you. There you will serve man-made gods of wood and stone, that cannot see or hear or eat or smell (Deuteronomy 4:27-28).

The Lord will scatter you among all the peoples from one end of the earth to the other, and there you shall serve other gods, wood and stone, whom neither you nor your ancestors have experienced (Deuteronomy 28:64).

Jeremiah echoes this theme:

Therefore I will hurl you out of this land to a land that neither you nor your fathers have known, and there you will serve other gods, day and night; for I will show you no mercy (Jeremiah 16:13).

Of course, the Israelites will not be required to worship idols, and never should worship idols while in exile. Nonetheless, exile to the lands of pagans makes them vulnerable to such worship.[16]

SUMMARY

There are no biblical holidays to commemorate Israel's entry into the land. The Torah thus creates a national covenantal identity that transcends the Land of Israel. Joshua's ceremony of acceptance of the Torah after the people entered the land teaches that faithfulness to God lies at the heart of Israel's remaining in its land. The Talmud adds that the Torah's vision also looks outward to all humanity, as Israel has a role to play in building a model society and inspiring the nations of the world to the Torah's level of religious morality.

David and Solomon establish Jerusalem as God's capital in ruling the world as well as the political capital of Israel. The Temple reenacts the Revelation at Sinai, and also functions as a taste of the Garden of Eden. Solomon expresses the vision of the Torah, that the Temple is open to all God-fearing people, and not only to Israel. Solomon's reign reflects the messianic age.

Tragically, the sin of idolatry contributed to the division of the monarchy, the exile of the ten Northern tribes, and ultimately the exile of Judah along with the destruction of the Temple. God's very creation had come undone, and the Israelites returned to Babylonia and Egypt, reversing the journeys of Abraham and Moses. The people thought that the God-Israel covenant had come to an end.

It required prophetic vision to look beyond the dark reality of the destruction and exile. Prophets proclaimed that the exile was a separation from God, not a permanent divorce. Israel might feel dead, but God will revive them. The Patriarchal covenant is in full, eternal force, and God will restore the Eden-like state of Israel. God also must redeem the people of Israel, as their exile desecrates God's Name. While in exile, the people must build institutions to retain their identity. But they always will return home to Israel.

The agricultural bounty of Israel, so prominently featured in the Torah, becomes an essential component of Israel's redemption. Ultimately, Israel once again will serve as the religious-moral epicenter of the world, and will restore the harmony of the Garden of Eden.

The Land of Israel is holy in the sense that only there is the God-Israel covenant fully attainable. Conversely, the lands outside of Israel are considered "unclean" because a full holy life is unattainable.

IV

ISRAEL IN THE SECOND TEMPLE
PERIOD AND IN THE CONTEMPORARY PERIOD

A MIRACLE OF HISTORY

Despite the intense despair of the people in the wake of the destruction of the Temple and the exile, Jeremiah offered a prophetic vision beyond the misery. There would be a full restoration to the land, but in the interim the Jews would need to build a strong Diaspora life:

> Thus said the Lord of Hosts, the God of Israel, to the whole community which I exiled from Jerusalem to Babylon: Build houses and live in them, plant gardens and eat their fruit. Take wives and beget sons and daughters; and take wives for your sons, and give your daughters to husbands, that they may bear sons and daughters. Multiply there, do not decrease. And seek the welfare of the city to which I have exiled you and pray to the Lord in its behalf; for in its prosperity you shall prosper.... For thus said the Lord: When Babylon's seventy years are over, I will take note of you, and I will fulfill to you My promise of favor—to bring you back to this place (Jeremiah 29:4-10).

After generations of exile, the nation experienced a shocking turn of events. Approximately seventy years after its inception, the seemingly invincible Babylonian Empire suddenly collapsed in the wake of the Persian onslaught under Cyrus. Even more remarkably, Cyrus permitted the Jews to return to Israel and rebuild the Temple. All of a sudden, the once seemingly impossible prophecies of Jeremiah were being realized before the people's eyes. The Book of Ezra opens with a reference to Jeremiah's prophecies, celebrating this miracle of history:

> In the first year of King Cyrus of Persia, when the word of the Lord spoken by Jeremiah was fulfilled, the Lord roused the spirit of King Cyrus of Persia to issue a proclamation throughout his realm by word of mouth and in writing as follows: "Thus said King Cyrus of Persia: The Lord God of Heaven has given me all the kingdoms of the earth and has charged me with building Him a house in Jerusalem, which is in Judah. Anyone of you of all His people—may his God be with him, and let him go up to Jerusalem that is in Judah and build the House of the Lord God of Israel, the God that is in Jerusalem; and all who stay behind, wherever he may be living, let the people of his place assist him with silver, gold, goods, and livestock, besides the freewill offering to the House of God that is in Jerusalem" (Ezra 1:1-4).

Ezra chapter 2 contains a lengthy list of the people who returned to Israel. The extensive coverage gives the initial impression that the Jewish response to Cyrus' permission to return was overwhelmingly positive. This impression is diminished by the fact that only 42,360 people returned (Ezra 2:64). Evidently, most Jews chose to remain in exile.

ZECHARIAH'S VISION OF A WALL OF FIRE SURROUNDING JERUSALEM

The prophet Zechariah received a series of visions to encourage the Jews to complete the rebuilding of the Second Temple. One element he addressed was the shame people felt over the walls of Jerusalem, which continued to be breached after the Babylonian invasion:

I looked up, and I saw a man holding a measuring line. "Where are you going?" I asked. "To measure Jerusalem," he replied, "to see how long and wide it is to be." But the angel who talked with me came forward, and another angel came forward to meet him. The former said to him, "Run to that young man and tell him: 'Jerusalem shall be peopled as a city without walls, so many shall be the men and cattle it contains. And I Myself—declares the Lord—will be a wall of fire all around it, and I will be a glory inside it'" (Zechariah 2:5-9).

Zechariah challenged the public perception of the broken walls of Jerusalem as being shameful, as later reported in the Book of Nehemiah:

They replied, "The survivors who have survived the captivity there in the province are in dire trouble and disgrace; Jerusalem's wall is full of breaches, and its gates have been destroyed by fire" (Nehemiah 1:3).

Then I said to them, "You see the bad state we are in—Jerusalem lying in ruins and its gates destroyed by fire. Come, let us rebuild the wall of Jerusalem and suffer no more disgrace" (Nehemiah 2:17).

In Zechariah's vision, the breached walls presented an opportunity to expand the borders of the city through a massive population increase. Instead of requiring physical walls for security, God would serve as a wall of fire to protect His people.

Prophecies are not fulfilled automatically. People need to do their part to realize the potential of the moment.[17] In this spirit, Zechariah immediately follows his vision with a call to the Jews still living in Babylonia:

"Away, away! Flee from the land of the north—says the Lord—though I swept you [there] like the four winds of heaven—declares the Lord." Away, escape, O Zion, you who dwell in Fair Babylon.... The Lord will take Judah to Himself as His portion in the Holy Land,[18] and He will choose Jerusalem once more (Zechariah 2:10-16).

If the people want Jerusalem's population to expand beyond the city walls, then the exiles need to leave Babylonia *en masse* and move to Israel!

Zechariah also prophesies that God will personally purify the land from its stains of sin:

I will remove that country's guilt in a single day (Zechariah 3:9).

In Zechariah chapter 5, the prophet explains that God will eliminate sinners, and then sin itself from the land.[19] In our discussions of the Land of Israel in the Torah, we observed that there is no ritual to purify the land from severe sin. Only exile of the sinners and God's intervention can allow the land proper opportunity to recover. God's Presence and the people now can return to a restored land.

Unfortunately, most Jews ignored Zechariah's call to return and chose to remain in exile. The ideal vision never was fulfilled. In the final analysis, Jerusalem was better off with a wall. Approximately 75 years after Zechariah's prophecy, Nehemiah rebuilt the walls of Jerusalem (445 BCE). The city was so desolate that he decreed that one-tenth of the Jewish community must resettle in Jerusalem so that it would remain a viable city (Nehemiah 11:1-2).

Within two generations of exile, there was a severe change in the mentality of the Jews. Those who had been exiled feared that the God-Israel relationship was over, and they could not even envision praying to God while in exile: "How can we sing a song of the Lord on alien soil?" (Psalm 137:4). Two generations later, most Jews were comfortable remaining in exile. They lived a robust life in the Diaspora, and evidently no longer perceived the exile as the supreme punishment of the Torah. As we discussed concerning the book of Genesis, Jacob also chose to remain at Laban's house for another six years after building his family to earn wages. There is nothing wrong with earning a living, but Jacob fell short of his covenantal responsibilities. Similarly, the family of Joseph remained in Egypt even after the famine, paving the way for the slavery under the following Pharaoh.

In the Tanakh, exile is described *exclusively* as a punishment for sin. However, several later rabbinic writers attempt to ascertain positive religious meaning in the exile. For example, Rabbi Yehudah Halevi in his *Kuzari* suggests that exile affords Jews the opportunity to influence other people. This kind of interpretation makes the most out of a negative situation, rather than expressing an ideal state of affairs.[20]

Putting the evidence together, the Talmud views the Second Temple period as a missed opportunity for the full messianic redemption:

> Similarly it has been taught: "Till Your people pass over, O Lord, till the people pass over that You have gotten" (Exodus 15:16). "Till Your people pass over, O Lord": this is the first entry [into the Land]. "Till the people pass over that You have acquired": this is the second entry. Hence the Sages say: The intention was to perform a miracle for Israel in the days of Ezra, even as it was performed for them in the days of Joshua bin Nun, but sin caused [the miracle to be withheld] (*Berakhot* 4a).

This passage does not specify what sin(s) withheld the full redemption. Several rabbinic sources maintain that the Jews' collective failure to return to the land prevented the full redemption from being realized:

> If she be a wall, we will build upon her a turret of silver; if she be a door, we will enclose her with boards of cedar. Had you made yourself like a wall and had all come up in the days of Ezra, you would have been compared to silver, which no rottenness can ever affect. Now that you have come up like doors, you are like cedarwood, which rottenness prevails over (*Yoma* 9b; cf. *Kuzari* II:24).

Simultaneously, the very existence of the Second Temple and a flourishing Jewish community in Israel convincingly demonstrated that the God-Israel relationship endures beyond the exile and is eternal. Malachi invokes the rebuilding of the land as a sign of God's abiding love of Israel:

> I have shown you love, said the Lord. But you ask, "How have You shown us love?" After all—declares the Lord—Esau is Jacob's brother; yet I have accepted Jacob and have rejected Esau. I have made his hills a desolation, his territory a home for beasts of the desert. If Edom thinks, "Though crushed, we can build the ruins again," thus said the Lord of Hosts: They may build, but I will tear down. And so they shall be known as the region of wickedness, the people damned forever of the Lord. Your eyes shall behold it, and you shall declare, "Great is the Lord beyond the borders of Israel!" (Malachi 1:2-5).

Similarly, the leaders during the religious revival under Ezra and Nehemiah highlight God's eternal covenant with Abraham and his descendants:

You are the Lord God, who chose Abram, who brought him out of Ur of the Chaldeans and changed his name to Abraham. Finding his heart true to You, You made a covenant with him to give the land of the Canaanite, the Hittite, the Amorite, the Perizzite, the Jebusite, and the Girgashite—to give it to his descendants. And You kept Your word, for You are righteous (Nehemiah 9:7-8).

PROFESSOR YEHUDAH ELITZUR

Professor Yehudah Elitzur[21] wrote from the vantage point of Jews returning to Israel after nearly 2000 years of exile, rather than simply after seventy years of Babylonian exile. This afforded him a broader perspective of the biblical passages.

In an essay on the religious significance of the Land of Israel in the Bible, Professor Elitzur reiterates the eternality of the covenant of the land alongside the threat of exile for unfaithfulness. Even if there would be an exile, no other nation will settle permanently in Israel. The land eternally belongs to Abraham's descendants:

I assign the land you sojourn in to you and your offspring to come, all the land of Canaan, as an everlasting holding. I will be their God (Genesis 17:8).

The ingathering of Jewish exiles to Israel in the contemporary period is a fulfillment of God's promise to Abraham that the land is an everlasting holding.

Lands typically do not remain desolate when they are conquered. Normally, other people occupy them. However, God promises that the Land of Israel would remain desolate if the people go into exile:

I will make the land desolate, so that your enemies who settle in it shall be appalled by it. And you I will scatter among the nations, and I will unsheathe the sword against you. Your land shall become a desolation and your cities a ruin (Leviticus 26:32-33).

In the ancient halakhic Midrash *Sifra*, the Sages remark that the uninhabited land is a positive dimension within this prophecy of doom. The land remains uninhabited so that Jews could return to an empty land.

In the thirteenth century, Ramban witnessed the desolation in Israel when he moved there toward the end of his life. He understood this desolation as proof of God's promise that the land eternally belongs to the Jews, and that God would return them to Israel one day:

[The desolation] constitutes a good tiding, proclaiming that during all our exiles, our land will not accept our enemies.... Since the time that we left it, [the land] has not accepted any nation or people, and they all try to settle it... This is a great proof and assurance to us (Ramban on Leviticus 26:16).

In the nineteenth century, Mark Twain was flabbergasted by the fact that Israel was almost completely desolate. In his *Innocents Abroad*, he remarked:

Of all the lands there are for dismal scenery, I think Palestine must be the prince... Can the curse of the Deity beautify a land? Palestine sits in sackcloth and ashes. Over it broods the spell of a curse that has withered its fields and fettered its energies.

Professor Elitzur observes further that the Canaanites who lived in the land prior to the Israelites succeeded in exploiting the natural resources of the land:

> When the Lord your God brings you into the land that He swore to your fathers, Abraham, Isaac, and Jacob, to assign to you—great and flourishing cities that you did not build, houses full of all good things that you did not fill, hewn cisterns that you did not hew, vineyards and olive groves that you did not plant—and you eat your fill (Deuteronomy 6:10-11).

However, the Canaanites never became a unified nation. Joshua defeated 31 kings, each a ruler of an independent city-state. In contrast, the people of Israel formed a united nation, the only people ever to do so in Israel. Moreover, no nation after Israel could exploit the natural resources of the land. Instead, the land remained a barren wasteland for nearly 2000 years.

Professor Elitzur invokes another rule of history: All other exiled people either assimilate into the dominant culture of the host nation, or else they are dominant because they come in large groups and take over the culture of the new land (e.g., the British in America, the Spanish in Argentina).

Despite being a minority, the Jews never totally assimilated into their host nations. They also remained a minority and never were able to set up a Jewish land outside of Israel. The Torah's curse that the people of Israel would be scattered and downtrodden in exile contains a hidden blessing, since they would always remain outsiders and therefore return one day to Israel.

The Jewish people and the Land of Israel belong to one another, and *need* one another. When they are together, both land and people flourish. When they are separate, Jews suffer and the land lies desolate.

SUMMARY

At the beginning of the Second Temple period, the Jews were miraculously allowed to return to their land and rebuild the Temple. While many Jews did return, the vast majority chose to remain in exile. Instead of the full redemption occurring then, the opportunity was squandered. It appears that the non-return of many Jews contributed meaningfully to the failure to realize the messianic era.

Although the ideal age did not occur in the Second Temple period, the Jews realized that God's covenantal promises were indeed eternal. Their return to their land demonstrated God's abiding love and commitment to the people of Israel.

In the Torah, God promises that the Land of Israel is an everlasting holding for the people of Israel. The ingathering of exiles in the modern era, the land blooming after remaining desolate for nearly 2000 years, and the fact that the Jews never completely assimilated nor formed a dominant culture elsewhere all fulfill divine promises. These facts are unique in human history, all attesting to the eternality of God's promises.

We live in a miraculous age with the Jewish people returned to Israel after such a lengthy exile. We cannot know how everything will unfold without prophecy. However, we may derive several religious lessons from the biblical corpus: (1) The return of the Jewish people to Israel confirms the biblical covenantal promises dating back to Abraham. (2) It is a fulfillment of God's promise that the land would remain a barren wasteland in the absence of the Jews, and that it would flourish once again when the Jews return. (3) The people of Israel must be grateful to God for this gift, and never take sole credit for this remarkable achievement or for the rehabilitation of the land. (4) The modern State of Israel poses a challenge to world Jewry to live up to God's covenant through the Torah, and to participate in rebuilding the land.

NOTES

1. For further discussion, see Hayyim Angel, "'The Chosen People': An Ethical Challenge," in Angel, *Increasing Peace Through Balanced Torah Study. Conversations* 27 (New York: Institute for Jewish Ideas and Ideals, 2017), pp. 38-47.

2. Yehudah Elitzur, "The Land of Israel in Biblical Thought" (Hebrew), in Elitzur, *Yisrael VehaMikra: Mehkarim Geografiyim, Historiyim, VaHagotiyim,* ed. Yoel Elitzur and Amos Frisch (Ramat-Gan: Bar-Ilan University Press, 2000), pp. 262-263.

3. Jon D. Levenson, *Inheriting Abraham: The Legacy of the Patriarch in Judaism, Christianity, and Islam* (Princeton, NJ: Princeton University Press, 2012), p. 84.

4. Elhanan Samet, *Iyyunim BeParashot HaShavua* vol. 1 (first series) (Hebrew) ed. Ayal Fishler (Ma'aleh Adumim: Ma'aliyot Press, 2002), pp. 75-88.

5. Yehudah Kiel, *Da'at Mikra: Bereshit*, vol. 1 (Jerusalem: Mosad HaRav Kook, 1997). For a survey of traditional opinions, see Kiel, pp. 426-428.

6. Shlomo Riskin, *Torah Lights: Genesis* (Jerusalem: Urim, 2005), pp. 307–312.

7. See, for example, Jeremiah 2:7-8, 23; 7:30; 19:13; 32:34; Ezekiel 20:7, 18, 31; 22:3, 4; 23:7, 30; 36:18; 37:23.

8. See Elhanan Samet, *Iyyunim BeParashot HaShavua* vol. 1 (second series) (Hebrew) ed. Ayal Fishler (Ma'aleh Adumim: Ma'aliyot Press, 2004), pp. 90-91.

9. See, for example, Deuteronomy 5:16, 28; 6:10-11, 23; 7:13; 8:10; 9:4-6, 23; 10:11; 11:9, 17, 21, 25; 12:1, 9; 15:4, 7; 16:20; 17:4; 18:9; 19:1-2, 8, 10, 14; 20:16; 21:1, 23; 24:4; 25:15, 19; 26:1-11, 15.

10. See, for example, Deuteronomy 6:10, 23; 7:13; 10:11; 11:9, 21; 19:8; 26:3, 15.

11. Rabbi Joseph B. Soloveitchik, *Birkon Mesorat HaRav*, ed. David Hellman (New York: OU Press, 2016), pp. 11-12.

12. Uriel Simon, "Biblical Destinies: Conditional Promises," in *Jewish Bible Theology: Perspectives and Case Studies*, ed. Isaac Kalimi (Winona Lake, IN: Eisenbrauns, 2012), pp. 79-87.

13. Moshe Greenberg, *Understanding Exodus* (New York: Behrman House, 1969), pp. 9-17.

14. This prophecy is so powerful that the writers of the *Hatikvah* drew from it when composing what became Israel's national anthem. Ezekiel speaks of the exiles saying that "our hope is gone"–*avedah tikvatenu*. The anthem triumphantly responds, *od lo avedah tikvatenu*, "Our hope is still not lost!"

15. For a survey of later rabbinic interpretations of this passage, see Marc Saperstein, "The Land of Israel in Pre-Modern Jewish Thought: A History of Two Rabbinic Statements," in *The Land of Israel: Jewish Perspectives*, ed. Lawrence A. Hoffman (Notre Dame: University of Notre Dame Press, 1986), pp. 188-209.

16. Rashi and Rabbenu Bahya (on Deuteronomy 4:28) explain that by Israel serving their pagan captors, it is as though they serve their gods, also. Ramban understands the verse in the sense that living in exile at some level resembles idol-worship.

17. For further discussion of this principle, see Hayyim Angel, "Prophecy as Potential: The Consolations of Isaiah 1-12 in Context," in Angel, *Revealed Texts, Hidden Meanings: Finding the Religious Significance in Tanakh* (Jersey City, NJ: Ktav-Sephardic Publication Foundation, 2009), pp. 117-126.

18. This verse is the only time in all Tanakh where the Land of Israel is called the Holy Land. Harry M. Orlinsky observes that Christians preferred calling the Land of Israel "the Holy Land," whereas Jews preferred *Eretz Yisrael*. Only as Jews left their ghettos did some adopt the term "the Holy Land." The term "*Eretz Yisrael*" referring to the entire Land of Israel also is rare in Tanakh, found only in I Samuel 13:19; Ezekiel 27:17; 40:2; 47:18; and II Chronicles 34:7 ("The Biblical Concept of the Land of Israel: Cornerstone of the Covenant between God and Israel," in *The Land of Israel: Jewish Perspectives*, ed. Lawrence A. Hoffman [Notre Dame: University of Notre Dame Press, 1986], pp. 54-55, 64).

19. See further analysis of this passage in Hayyim Angel, *Haggai, Zechariah, and Malachi: Prophecy in an Age of Uncertainty* (Jerusalem: Maggid, 2016), pp. 66-70.

20. See further discussion and sources in Yehudah Elitzur, "The Meaning of Exile in the Bible" (Hebrew), in Elitzur, *Yisrael ve-ha-Mikra: Mehkarim*

Geografiyim, Historiyim, va-Hagotiyim, ed. Yoel Elitzur and Amos Frisch (Ramat-Gan: Bar-Ilan University Press, 2000), pp. 280-293.

21. Yehudah Elitzur, "The Land of Israel in Biblical Thought" (Hebrew), in Elitzur, *Yisrael ve-ha-Mikra: Mehkarim Geografiyim, Historiyim, va-Hagotiyim,* ed. Yoel Elitzur and Amos Frisch (Ramat-Gan: Bar-Ilan University Press, 2000), pp. 261-279.

IDEAL AND EVOLUTIONARY MORALITY IN THE TORAH

TRADITIONAL COMMENTARY IN AN AGE OF HUMANISM*

INTRODUCTION

One of the overarching goals of the Torah is to refine people's moral character. Many laws and narratives overtly focus on morality, and many others inveigh against the immorality and amorality of paganism. The biblical prophets place consistency between observance of God's ritual and moral laws at the very heart of their message.

Rabbi Saadiah Gaon insists that God chooses only good things to command. He rejects the position of the medieval Islamic school of *Ash'ariyya*, which maintained that whatever God commands is by definition good.[1]

Similarly, Rambam asserts that every commandment teaches justice and noble qualities, or corrects philosophical errors (*Guide* 3:27). Rambam cites God's desire to have all the nations of the world perceive the moral superiority of the Torah:

> Observe them faithfully, for that will be proof of your wisdom and discernment to other peoples, who on hearing of all these laws will say, "Surely, that great nation is a wise and discerning people." For what great nation is there that

* This article appeared originally in *Conversations* 33 (Winter 2019), pp. 38-52.

has a god so close at hand as is the Lord our God whenever we call upon Him? Or what great nation has laws and rules as perfect as all this Teaching that I set before you this day? (Deuteronomy 4:6-8).

Many other Jewish thinkers likewise adopt the position that the Torah promotes the highest moral values.

In recent generations, this position has been augmented with the discovery of many ancient Near Eastern laws and narratives. Leading scholars of the twentieth century demonstrated how the Torah promotes moral values vastly superior to those of the prevailing cultures of that day.[2] Contemporary writers also have verified the extent to which the Torah's values have exerted a decisive influence on contemporary Western morality.[3]

Contemporary readers, though, confront a troubling question. Does the Torah promote the *highest* morality? Several commandments appear to conflict with modern moral sentiments. Although there might not be unanimity on what contemporary moral sentiments are or should be, we can point to several areas that have attracted serious attention among traditional thinkers.

For example, the Torah permits slavery and polygamy. It permits the blood relatives of one who is killed accidentally to kill the manslayer if he or she fails to reach, or subsequently leaves, a city of refuge. The Torah commands the total eradication of the Canaanites and Amalekites. Granting that both societies were depraved and evil, and that these laws are not applicable today, God's stark commandment to kill men, women, and children remains in the Torah. There is a clash between the Torah's severe prohibition of homosexual relations and the sentiments of many people today. While the sacrificial order of the Temple raises different issues, it also is difficult for many in the modern era to fathom.

Over the past two centuries, Jewish thinkers have engaged in a thoughtful conversation about these and related issues. Some of these discussions have roots in ancient and medieval thought, but these questions have received far more attention in the modern era, driven at least in part by humanistic values. There is sufficient distance between the setting of the Torah and our setting, so that many today feel tensions in ways that earlier generations did not.

Rabbi Yaakov Medan, one of the Roshei Yeshiva at Yeshivat Har Etzion, rejects the dangerous fundamentalist approach that we must blindly draw our morality from Tanakh without further inquiry. He also rejects the position of Professor Yeshayahu Leibowitz (1903-1994), who insisted that there is no connection between God and morality, and that Jews simply must obey God's laws. Rabbi Medan states that there are two basic approaches for those who believe that the divinely revealed Torah is moral: (1) Apologetics, reconciling what we see in the text with our moral sentiments. This approach is dishonest, as it imposes the will of the reader onto the text. (2) Attempting to understand God's word on its own terms, while simultaneously retaining our own moral sense. God is beyond our comprehension, but we never stop struggling with these complex moral issues.[4]

In this essay, I adopt the latter view of Rabbi Medan. Although it is impossible to be objective, it appears that the evidence supports the notion of an evolutionary morality regarding certain tolerated practices. At the same time, the Torah's mandatory commandments may reflect realities of its ancient setting, but remain eternally binding as God's word. In the latter case, there is room for evolving interpretations of the law.

ANCIENT AND MEDIEVAL PRECEDENTS

Talmud: The Beautiful Captive

The Torah gives laws pertaining to a "beautiful captive" (*yefat to'ar*) taken in battle (Deuteronomy 21:10-14). Commentators debate the plain meaning of the biblical text. Some maintain that an Israelite soldier may have one-time sexual relations with her immediately at wartime (Rambam, *Hilkhot Melakhim* 8:2-7, Abarbanel), while others insist that the soldier first must wait thirty days and then decide if he still wants to marry her (Ibn Ezra, Ramban). The Talmud supports the former view, and therefore the one-time sexual union with the captive is permissible in *halakhah*. Why would God allow this act, instead of prohibiting it outright? The Talmud answers:

> With respect to the first intercourse there is universal agreement that it is permitted, since the Torah only provided for man's evil passions (*Kiddushin* 21b).

God would have outlawed this sexual union, but knew that many ancient soldiers would violate the prohibition. Therefore, God chose the lesser offense and permitted but discouraged the act by focusing on the humanity and humiliation of the captive. God thus legislated for a flawed human reality, provided a realistic law and circumscribed it, and simultaneously taught the ideal value and mode of conduct, to cultivate a society in which no soldier ever would perform this act.[5]

Rambam: Animal Sacrifices

Rambam maintains that God revealed many laws to wean the Israelites away from pagan culture to the service of God (*Guide* 3:29). Having spent so long in pagan Egypt, the Israelites had a strong predilection to offer animal sacrifices. God therefore instituted animal sacrifices. God further prescribed specific boundaries for this form of worship by insisting that animals could be sacrificed only in authorized shrines such as the Tabernacle or later the Temple. Prayer and contemplation, which are higher forms of serving God, thereby were encouraged as substitutes for animal sacrifices (*Guide* 3:32).

Ramban (on Leviticus 1:9) attacks Rambam on this assertion: "Behold, these words are worthless; they make a big breach, raise big questions, and pollute the table of God." He maintains that the Temple, sacrifices, and related laws are ideal means of communing with God, and not concessions to the ancient Israelites' historical setting.[6]

In addition, Rambam's view raised the fundamental question: Now that we have become more sophisticated, what would be the relevance of these ritual commandments in our times? Living in the nineteenth century, Rabbi Samson Raphael Hirsch lamented the terrible misapplication of Rambam's thought among assimilating German Jews. Many were using Rambam's logic in the *Guide* as precedent for abandoning other ritual commandments as well.[7] This concern did not originate with Rabbi Hirsch, as Rambam himself was concerned with the possibility of the masses' losing respect for many commandments if their reasons were revealed (*Guide* 3:26).[8]

Elsewhere in his writings, Rambam stresses the religious value of animal sacrifices (*Hilkhot Me'ilah* 8:8). He further maintains that in the messianic future, sacrifices will be restored with the rebuilding of the Temple (*Hilkhot Melakhim* 11:1). More broadly, Rambam maintains that all of the Torah's commandments are eternal, including into the messianic era (*Guide* 2:39; 3:34).[9] Rambam's placing sacrifices in their historical setting, then, never renders these laws obsolete.

To summarize, the Talmud discusses an instance where the Torah tolerates behavior as a concession to human weakness. Instead of outlawing the undesirable behavior, it circumscribes the action and makes it clear that one ideally should not do it at all. In Rambam's explanation of the rationale behind the Temple and sacrifices, the eternal observance of the commandments is absolute regardless of the time-bound aspect of the Torah responding to its ancient pagan setting. God developed an evolutionary educational program to teach Israel certain religious ideals over time.

Regarding conventions that the Torah permits, one may pit the Torah's ideal values against ancient social reality and explain that the Torah created an evolutionary program with the goal of eliminating certain practices that were too difficult to abolish at the time of God's revelation of the Torah to Moses. With mandatory commandments, we may change our interpretations of the reasons, but not the commandments themselves.

We now turn to a few examples where modern thinkers interpret certain tolerated practices of the Torah as parts of the Torah's evolutionary educational program for Israel and for humanity.

LESS-THAN-IDEAL ACTIONS TOLERATED BY THE TORAH

Polygamy

The Torah permits polygamy; yet one may argue that this permission was a concession to ancient reality and is distant from the Torah's ideal of monogamous relationships.

The Torah introduces the concept of a loving monogamous marriage at the very beginning of human existence:

> And the Lord God fashioned the rib that He had taken from the man into a woman; and He brought her to the man. Then the man said, "This one at last is bone of my bones and flesh of my flesh. This one shall be called Woman, for

from man was she taken." Hence a man leaves his father and mother and clings to his wife, so that they become one flesh (Genesis 2:22-24).

Biblical narratives that involve polygamy such as Abraham-Sarah-Hagar, Jacob-Rachel-Leah, and Elkanah-Hannah-Peninah invariably yield tension in the household. Tellingly, the biblical word for wife-in-law is *tzarah*, "tormentor" (I Samuel 1:6; Leviticus 18:18).

Given the Torah's ideal portrayal of a monogamous marriage in Eden, its negative portrayal of polygamy, and the fact that there is no mandatory commandment for a man to marry more than one wife, we may consider polygamy an institution that the Torah tolerated as a concession to ancient reality. A monogamous society is the Torah's ideal from its inception. The Torah set out its ideal values so that one day, they could be realized and polygamy would be abolished.

Blood Vengeance

The Torah permits a close relative to kill an accidental manslayer without trial. The manslayer must escape to the city of refuge and remain inside that city for safety (Numbers 35:9-34; Deuteronomy 19:1-13).

The nineteenth-century commentator Rabbi Samuel David Luzzatto (Shadal on Numbers 35:12) asks: Why does the Torah not simply outlaw vigilante justice and leave the matter to the courts? He suggests that the Torah presents a weaning process. In the ancient world, people would have felt like they did not love their deceased relative if they would refrain from killing the accidental manslayer. Even if the Torah would prohibit this behavior, many would violate the Torah anyway. Acknowledging that reality, the

Torah circumscribes blood vengeance by protecting the accidental manslayer and emphasizing his or her innocent blood. Ideally, the relatives should not engage in blood vengeance.

Professor Nehama Leibowitz (1905-1997) agrees with Shadal, and adds that the Torah succeeded in its evolutionary educational program. The talmudic Sages refer to going to the cities of refuge as "exile" (Mishnah *Makkot* 2:1), replacing the Torah's usage of the term "to flee" (Exodus 21:13; Numbers 35:15; Deuteronomy 19:5). Professor Leibowitz suggests that this change in terminology stems from the fact that the Torah eradicated the urge for blood vengeance. No longer did accidental manslayers "flee" the blood relatives out of fear being killed, but instead went into "exile" as a consequence of the Torah's legislation.[10]

Slavery

The Torah's legislation regarding slavery is vastly more humane than any other form of slavery in the ancient world.[11] And yet, why does the Torah permit slavery *at all*? Several recent rabbinic thinkers, including Rabbis Norman Lamm and Nahum Rabinovitch, discuss this phenomenon and reach similar conclusions.[12] The following is a brief amalgam of their views.

The ultimate goal of the Torah is for humanity to realize that slavery is wrong, and should be abolished. From Creation, the Torah teaches that all people derive from the same ancestry, and are created in God's image. However, humanity went astray. Men subjugated one another and distinguished between slaves and masters. When God revealed the Torah to Moses, the world economy depended on slavery, so the Torah could not realistically outlaw slavery. Rather, it taught society to advance step by step, until the goal of the elimination of slavery could be fully achieved.

Many laws remind Israel to care for the downtrodden of society, since the Israelites were slaves in Egypt. Shabbat gives a taste of the ideal world, where slaves rest also. While tolerating slavery, the Torah revolutionized the institution. It set a floor that prevented descent to the vile abuses practiced by other nations. Its ultimate goal is that over time, people should question why we have slaves at all. The abolition of slavery in most of the world today is a realization of the ideals taught by the Torah.[13]

To summarize, God responded to a flawed human reality by revealing laws that outlawed many ancient practices immediately, while tolerating—but also modifying and restricting—other undesirable practices with the goal of eliminating them over time. In an ideal world, God would not have permitted the taking of beautiful captives, polygamy, blood vengeance, or slavery. God tolerated these practices as concessions to ancient reality, and simultaneously taught ideal morality so that Israel and humanity could evolve and abolish these practices over time. The fact that many people today consider these practices morally unacceptable is a tribute to the success of the Torah's long-term educational vision of ideal divine law.

CONFLICTS BETWEEN MANDATORY COMMANDMENTS AND CONTEMPORARY MORAL SENTIMENTS

Sacrifices and Other Temple Rituals

As discussed above, Rambam viewed the Temple and its sacrifices as a necessary aspect of God's evolutionary approach to reaching the ideal society. Ancient Israelites were unable to receive a religious system devoid of a Temple and its sacrificial rites. Yet, Rambam also wrote that the Temple will be rebuilt and sacrifices restored in the messianic era (*Hilkhot Melakhim* 11:1). This position is no different from Rambam's suggestion that the prohibition of cooking a kid in its mother's milk also served to wean Israel away from pagan practices (*Guide* 3:48), yet those laws are fully applicable for all time.

Beyond Rambam's general view on the eternality of the Torah's commandments, Professor Menachem Kellner offers additional reasons why the restoration of sacrifices is critical for Rambam's position on the messianic era. Rambam's messianism is non-supernatural, and idolatry is an ever-present threat even in the messianic era. Therefore, sacrifices are necessary to continue to wean humanity away from the immorality and foolishness of paganism. Additionally, the messianic era is restorative, returning all institutions from the time of David and Solomon to their former glory. The reinstitution of the Temple, sacrifices, and the Sabbatical and Jubilee years are central to that vision.[14]

Professor Micah Goodman adds that Rambam maintains that Abraham's religion without commandments failed to preserve his philosophical monotheism long term among his descendants (*Hilkhot Avodat Kokhavim* 1:1-3). Absent rituals, God's ideal religious values cannot endure in society. Rituals that uphold group identity and reinforce its core principles are required for long-term survival and religious flourishing (cf. *Guide* 2:31).[15]

Despite what appears to be Rambam's position, some extend Rambam's approach and conclude that there will not be sacrifice in the messianic future. One contemporary thinker who has expressed his struggle from different perspectives is Rabbi Nathan Lopes Cardozo. In one article, he concludes that were God to reveal the Torah today, it would not include laws of slavery or sacrifices:

> [N]ot only would the laws concerning sacrifices and slavery be
> totally abolished once the people outgrew the need for them,

but they would actually not have appeared in the biblical text had it been revealed at a much later stage in Jewish history.[16]

Rabbi Cardozo makes no distinction between the Torah's toleration of slavery, which is not commanded; and sacrifices, which are mandatory commandments. He does not address Rambam's other writings that insist on the eternality of all of the Torah's commandments or that the sacrificial order will be restored in the messianic era. Rabbi Cardozo's leap from tolerated practices to mandatory commandments appears to go beyond the evidence in the Torah and in Rambam's writings.

In a different essay,[17] Rabbi Cardozo restates his position that the Torah contains concessions to human weakness, and sets out an evolutionary road toward higher forms of worship. What of Rambam's ruling that the sacrifices will be restored in the messianic era? Rabbi Cardozo submits, "I believe he thus expresses his doubt that the *ought-to-be* of Judaism will ever become a reality in this world."[18] This position resonates with the view of Professor Kellner stated above, that Rambam maintains that the idolatrous urge will remain even in the messianic era so sacrifices will be necessary to counteract that urge.

To summarize, Rambam maintains that the laws of the Torah are eternal, and that the Temple and sacrifices will be restored in the messianic future. The law remains unchanged, but the religious meaning one ascribes to the commandments can change. When the messianic era arrives, we will be in a better position to judge what actually will happen.[19]

Homosexuality

A similar approach can apply to the Torah's unequivocal prohibition against male homosexual relations. The prohibition is unchangeable, but there has been a meaningful evolution within rabbinic responses in certain sectors of the contemporary Orthodox community. While there remains a wide range of opinion and approach within the Orthodox rabbinate and community, it is encouraging to see these more inclusive positions.[20]

War Against Canaan

Granting that the Canaanites and Amalekites were depraved and evil, the Torah's commandment to exterminate their populations—men, women, and children—remains stark. A full discussion of this issue goes beyond the parameters of this essay. It is noteworthy that of our medieval commentators, only Rabbenu Bahya (fourteenth century) raised the moral question of the Torah's command to kill even the children. His answers likely would not satisfy modern sentiments: It was a divine decree; once God decrees their doom they are considered as dead; they no doubt will grow up to be like their parents. Rabbenu Bahya makes the analogy to amputating a limb to save the body: the elimination of Canaanites and Amalekites was good for humanity.[21]

It is not until the twentieth century that rabbinic thinkers began to address this moral question more systematically.[22] Rabbi Abraham Isaac Kook (1865-1935) maintains that this commandment was restricted to the biblical period, and reflects ancient conventions of warfare. If Israel did not eliminate the Canaanites and Amalekites, they would regroup and attack Israel. The only way to stop enemies in an immoral world is to subdue them completely. As the moral expectations of the world regarding war improve, Israel must follow the highest moral standards and not apply the rules of the war against Canaanites and Amalekites (*Iggerot HaRei'ah* 1:89).

Rabbi Kook thus understands the parameters of the Torah's commandment as God's recognition of the reality of the ancient world. The Oral Law enables later generations to improve moral standards, rather than remaining fixated on the ancient standards of war and applying them in later periods.[23]

Rambam vs. Abarbanel on Monarchy

We have discussed the distinction between less-than-ideal non-mandatory practices that the Torah tolerated versus commandments where interpretations change while the law is eternal. One debate that proves this rule is the disagreement between Rambam and Abarbanel regarding monarchy (Deuteronomy 17:14-20).

Rambam considers monarchy to be a positive commandment (*Hilkhot Melakhim* 1:1–2). Abarbanel rejects Rambam's view based on several textual considerations and maintains that although monarchy is permitted if requested, it is viewed negatively by the Torah. Abarbanel likens monarchy to the laws of the "beautiful captive" (Deuteronomy 21:10–14), where the Torah tolerates certain less-than-ideal actions to forestall worse eventualities. He invokes the talmudic principle discussed earlier in this essay, "the Torah states this in consideration of the evil inclination" (*Kiddushin* 21b).[24]

Monarchy reflected the prevalent form of government in Israel's ancient setting. The Torah and the people in Samuel's time explicitly state that Israel wanted a king "as do all the nations" (Deuteronomy 17:14; I Samuel 8:5). For Rambam, however, the Torah commands this form of government so it transcends that ancient setting and is mandatory whenever it is politically feasible. For Abarbanel, monarchy is a tolerated negative practice until such time as people develop alternative forms of government.[25]

CONCLUSION

The prophets and ancient and medieval rabbinic thinkers recognized the centrality of ethics in the Torah's vision and law. In the modern era, many traditional thinkers perceived a growing gap between the morality of some of the Torah's laws and the ideal morals of Western humanism.

The talmudic analysis of the beautiful captive (*Kiddushin* 21b) provides the precedent for later thinkers to develop the concept that the Torah occasionally tolerates a less-than-ideal reality as a concession to ancient mores. Rambam's discussion of the Temple and sacrifices provides the precedent for later thinkers to propose new meanings to eternal commandments.

For matters that the Torah tolerates but does not command, such as polygamy, blood vengeance, and slavery, one may ascertain a gap between the Torah's tolerance and its ideal to abolish these practices. For mandatory commandments, such as a Temple and sacrifices and the prohibition against male homosexual relations, the laws are eternal but there remains room for different interpretations of these commandments so that our attitudes and religious-moral experience can evolve with time.

This essay outlines several areas that have drawn the attention of modern thinkers. These discussions are a healthy and vital aspect of our relationship with God and our desire to live in accordance with the Torah's ideal moral values.

The world has a long way to go to realize the messianic ideal. We pray for a growing embodiment of the Torah's ideals: A loving faithful marriage as the central bond for raising a family and transmitting religious values; a universal commitment to law and justice; a realization that all human beings are created in God's image, with no racism, sexism, or other forms of discrimination; a universal desire to connect to God through living a life of holiness; and a world where all evil is eliminated, and humanity serves God and lives ideal moral lives.

NOTES

1. Howard Kreisel, *Prophecy: The History of an Idea in Medieval Jewish Philosophy* (Dordrecht, Boston: Kluwer Academic Publishers, 2001), p. 38. See also Rabbi Aharon Lichtenstein, "Does Jewish Tradition Recognize an Ethics Independent of Halakha?" in *Contemporary Jewish Ethics*, ed. Menachem Kellner (New York: Sanhedrin Press, 1978), pp. 102-123.

2. See Moshe Greenberg, "Some Postulates of Biblical Criminal Law," and "The Biblical Concept of Asylum," in Moshe Greenberg, *Studies in the Bible and Jewish Thought* (Philadelphia: Jewish Publication Society, 1995), pp. 25-50; Nahum M. Sarna, *Exploring Exodus: The Origins of Biblical Israel* (New York: Schocken, 1996), pp. 158-189. For a summary of the current state of scholarship and a discussion of religious implications pertaining to the comparison of the Torah to ancient Near Eastern literature, see Amnon Bazak, *Ad HaYom HaZeh, Until this Day: Fundamental Questions in Bible Teaching*, ed. Yoshi Farajun (Hebrew) (Tel-Aviv: Yediot Aharonot-Hemed, 2013), pp. 317-346.

3. See, for example, Joshua Berman, *Created Equal: How the Bible Broke with Ancient Political Thought* (Oxford: Oxford University Press, 2008); Jeremiah Unterman, *Justice for All: How the Bible Revolutionized Ethics* (Philadelphia: Jewish Publication Society, 2017); *Proclaim Liberty Throughout the Land: The Hebrew Bible in the United States: A Sourcebook*, ed. Stuart W. Halpern, *et al.* (New Milford, CT: Toby Press, 2019).

4. Yaakov Medan, *HaMikraot HaMithaddeshim* (Hebrew) (Alon Shevut: Tevunot, 2015), pp. 255-349, especially pp. 255-265. See also Eugene Korn, "Moralization in Jewish Law: Genocide, Divine Commands, and Rabbinic Reasoning," *Edah Journal* 5:2 (2006), at http://www.edah.org/backend/JournalArticle/KORN_5_2.pdf. Accessed June 19, 2018.

5. See further discussion in Rabbi Mordechai Sabbato, "The Female Captive: What is the Torah Teaching Us?" at https://www.etzion.org.il/en/female-captive-what-torah-teaching-us, accessed March 21, 2019.

6. For analysis of the debate between Rambam and Ramban, and of the apparent contradictions within Rambam's writings on the subject

of animal sacrifice, see Russell Jay Hendel, "Maimonides' Attitude Towards Sacrifices," *Tradition* 13:4-14:1 (Spring-Summer, 1973), pp. 163-179; David Henshke, "On the Question of Unity in Rambam's Thought" (Hebrew), *Da'at* 37 (1996), pp. 37-51.

7. See the eighteenth of Rabbi Hirsch's *Nineteen Letters*. Russel Jay Hendel observes: "Rabbi Hirsch praises the Rambam for preserving medieval Judaism but also severely criticizes him for the effect the *Moreh's* views were having at Rabbi Hirsch's time. There is a difference in tone between the Ramban and Rabbi Hirsch. Ramban although using quite strong language, nevertheless is basically criticizing the *view* of the Rambam. Rabbi Hirsch however criticizes the *methodology* of the Rambam" ("Maimonides' Attitude Towards Sacrifices," p. 179, n. 48).

8. See Isadore Twersky, *Introduction to the Code of Maimonides (Mishneh Torah)* (New Haven: Yale University Press, 1980), pp. 374-484; David Henshke, "On the Question of Unity in Rambam's Thought."

9. See survey and discussion of the views of Rambam and other rabbinic thinkers in Marc B. Shapiro, *The Limits of Orthodox Theology: Maimonides' Thirteen Principles Reappraised* (Oxford: The Littman Library of Jewish Civilization, 204), pp. 122-131.

10. Nehama Leibowitz, *Studies in Devarim-Deuteronomy* (Jerusalem: Eliner Library), pp. 187-194.

11. For detailed analysis, see Elhanan Samet, *Iyyunim BeParashot HaShavua* (second series) vol. 1 (Hebrew) ed. Ayal Fishler (Ma'aleh Adumim: Ma'aliyot Press, 2004), pp. 377-397.

12. Norman Lamm, "Amalek and the Seven Nations: A Case of Law vs. Morality," in *War and Peace in the Jewish Tradition*, ed. Lawrence Schiffman and Joel B. Wolowelsky (New York: Yeshiva University Press, 2007), pp. 201–238. Nahum Rabinovitch, "The Way of Torah," *Edah Journal* 3:1 (Tevet 5763), at http://www.edah.org/backend/ coldfusion/search/document.cfm?title=The%20Way%20of%20 Torah&hyperlink=rabin3_1%2Ehtm&type=JournalArticle& category=Orthodoxy%20and%20Modernity&authortitle=& firstname=Nahum%20Eliezer%20&lastname=Rabinovitch&

pubsource=not%20available&authorid=335&pdfattachment=
Rabinovitch3_1%2Epdf. Accessed June 19, 2018.

13. For a survey of other modern rabbinic approaches to slavery, see
    Gamliel Shmalo, "Orthodox Approaches to Biblical Slavery," *The
    Torah u-Madda Journal* 16 (2012-2013), pp. 1-20.

14. Menachem Kellner, "'And the Crooked Shall be Made Straight':
    Twisted Messianic Visions, and a Maimonidean Corrective," in
    Rethinking the Messianic Idea in Judaism, ed. Michael L. Morgan and
    Steven Weitzman (Bloomington: Indiana University Press, 2015),
    pp. 108-140 (I thank Professor Kellner for this reference). See also
    Moshe Halbertal, *Maimonides: Life and Thought*, trans. Joel Linsider
    (Princeton: Princeton University Press, 2014), pp. 223-228, 341-353;
    Aviezer Ravitsky, "'To the Utmost of Human Capacity': Maimonides
    on the Days of the Messiah," in *Perspectives on Maimonides: Philosophical
    and Historical Studies*, ed. Joel L. Kraemer (Oxford: Littman Library
    of Jewish Civilization, 1996), pp. 221-256; Netanel Wiederblank,
    *Illuminating Jewish Thought: Explorations of Free Will, the Afterlife, and the
    Messianic Era* (Jerusalem: Maggid, 2018), pp. 547-556.

15. Micah Goodman, *Maimonides and the Book that Changed Judaism: Secrets
    of the Guide for the Perplexed* (Philadelphia: Jewish Publication Society,
    2015), pp. 113-137.

16. Nathan Lopes Cardozo, "The Deliberately Flawed Divine Torah," at
    http://thetorah.com/the-deliberately-flawed-divine-torah/, accessed
    June 21, 2018.

17. Nathan Lopes Cardozo, *Jewish Law as Rebellion: A Plea for Religious
    Authenticity and Halachic Courage* (Jerusalem: Urim, 2018), pp. 219-223.

18. See Rabbi Cardozo's further exploration of this idea in his book,
    Between Silence and Speech: Essays on Jewish Thought (Northvale, NJ:
    Jason Aronson, 1995), pp. 1-12.

19. In his commentary on the prayer book, Rabbi Abraham Isaac Kook
    suggests that in the messianic future, there will be only flour sacri-
    fices, and no more animal sacrifice (*Olat Re'iyah*, 292; cf. Rabbi Kook's
    LeNevukhei HaDor, chapter 10, where he suggests that if righteous peo-
    ple in the messianic era are unwilling to bring animal sacrifice, it is

within the right of the Sanhedrin then to reinterpret the Torah so that only flour sacrifices will be offered). However, Rabbi Kook's view is more complex based on his other writings. See Netanel Wiederblank, *Illuminating Jewish Thought*, pp. 557-572. See also Rabbi Haim David Halevy, *Asei Lekha Rav* 9:36, who espoused a similar position to that of Rabbi Kook in *Olat Re'iyah*. However, Rabbi Halevy elsewhere also insisted that the full sacrificial order will be restored in the messianic future. For analysis of Rabbi Halevy's position, see Marc D. Angel and Hayyim Angel, *Rabbi Haim David Halevy: Gentle Scholar and Courageous Thinker* (Jerusalem: Urim, 2006), pp. 85-87. For a few other recent rabbis who suggested that there will not be animal sacrifices in the messianic future, see Marc B. Shapiro, *The Limits of Orthodox Theology*, pp. 128-130.

20. For an excellent formulation of the inclusive position, see the Statement of Principles on the Place of Jews with a Homosexual Orientation in Our Community, at http://statementofprinciplesnya.blogspot.com/, accessed June 21, 2018. More broadly, see Chaim Rapoport, *Judaism and Homosexuality: An Authentic Orthodox View* (London: Vallentine Mitchell, 2004).

21. See Menachem Kellner, "And Yet, the Texts Remain," in *The Gift of the Land and the Fate of the Canaanites in Jewish Thought* (New York: Oxford University Press, 2014), pp. 153-179.

22. See Hayyim Angel, "War Against Canaan: Divine and Human Perspectives," in Angel, *Vision from the Prophet and Counsel from the Elders: A Survey of Nevi'im and Ketuvim* (New York: OU Press, 2013), pp. 41-48; Yoel Bin-Nun, "*HaMikra BeMabat Histori VehaHitnahlut HaYisraelit BeEretz Cena'an*" (Hebrew), in *HaPulmus al HaEmet HaHistorit BaMikra*, ed. Yisrael L. Levin and Amihai Mazar (Yad Yitzhak Ben Zvi, Merkaz Dinur: 2002), pp. 3-16; Yoel Bin-Nun, "*Sefer Yehoshua–Peshat VeDivrei Hazal*" (Hebrew), in *Musar Milhamah VeKibush* (Alon Shevut: Tevunot, 1994), pp. 31-40; Shalom Carmy, "The Origin of Nations and the Shadow of Violence: Theological Perspectives on Canaan and Amalek," in *War and Peace in the Jewish Tradition*, pp. 163–199; Yaakov Medan, *HaMikraot HaMithaddeshim*, pp. 255-349.

23. See further discussion in Amnon Bazak, *Ad HaYom HaZeh*, pp. 404-417. It is noteworthy that only in the nineteenth century did Malbim raise the moral question of the mutilation (rather than quick execution) of Adoni-Bezek. Earlier generations of classical commentators did not.

24. For further discussion, see Hayyim Angel, "Abarbanel: Commentator and Teacher: Celebrating 500 Years of his Influence on Tanakh Study," in Angel, *Peshat Isn't So Simple: Essays on Developing a Religious Methodology to Bible Study* (New York: Kodesh Press, 2014), pp. 80-104.

25. Consistent with his position, Rambam maintained that monarchy will return to Israel in the messianic era (*Hilkhot Melakhim* 11:1). Scholars debate whether Abarbanel believed that there will be a monarchy in the messianic era. Yitzhak Baer and Leo Strauss maintained that Abarbanel believed that the messianic leader would function as a king for the nations but not for the Jews, a situation resembling the biblical period of the Judges. However, Eric Lawee observes that Abarbanel is explaining the position of Rabbi Hillel in the Talmud, rather than explicitly expressing his own personal view. It therefore is possible that Abarbanel himself expected some form of limited monarchy in the messianic era. For discussion and references, see Eric Lawee, *Isaac Abarbanel's Stance Toward Tradition: Defense, Dissent, and Dialogue* (New York: SUNY Press, 2001), pp. 137-141 and pp. 266-267, notes 62, 70. I thank Professor Lawee for this reference. See further discussion in Gerald Blidstein, "Halakha and Democracy," *Tradition* 32:1 (Fall 1997), pp. 6-39. I thank Professor Menachem Kellner for this reference.

TANAKH AND SUPERSTITION

DEBATES WITHIN TRADITIONAL COMMENTARY*

The Torah rooted out many ancient pagan superstitions. Professor Yehezkel Kaufmann (1889-1963) pinpointed several critical features that fundamentally distinguish Tanakh from ancient Near Eastern literature. There is one supreme God above who is the Creator of all nature, and there are no forces competing with God. God is absolutely free. God is timeless, ageless, nonphysical, and eternal. Nature is a stage on which God expresses His will in history. Rituals do not harness independent magical powers and do not work automatically. Endowed with free will, people can defy God and even drive God's Presence away. Evil does not inhere in universe but rather is a product of people sinning, and it undermines creation. Absolute standards of good and justice exist, and people may use their free will to build an ideal society.[1]

The overwhelming majority of Tanakh fits this description perfectly. God and human behavior are responsible for nearly all events. This premise is so self-evident that one Mishnah dismisses any possibility of a "magical" reading of two Torah narratives that could have been read that way: Moses' raised arms assisting Israel in the battle against Amalek (Exodus 17:8-16); and Moses' using a divinely-commanded brass serpent to heal serpent-bitten Israelites in the wilderness (Numbers 21:4-9):

---

* This essay appeared originally in *Conversations* 35 (Spring 2020), pp. 14-28.

Is it Moses' hands that make or break success in war? Rather, this comes to tell you, that whenever Israel looked upward and subjugated their hearts to their Father in heaven, they would prevail. If not, they would fall. Similarly, you can say concerning the verse, "Make a [graven] snake and place it on a pole, and everyone bitten who sees it will live." Is it the snake that kills or revives? Rather, whenever Israel looked upward and subjugated their hearts to their Father in heaven, they would be healed. If not, they would be harmed (Mishnah, *Rosh Hashanah* 3:8).

There are instances, however, where some commentators interpret biblical narratives and laws in ways that differ from the above principles. This essay focuses on biblical passages that could be interpreted as reflecting powers that do not directly emanate from God. Among traditional commentators, there is diversity of opinion regarding the existence of forces beyond the divine. In most cases, Tanakh does not exhibit evidence of forces beyond God's realm, but there are a few occasions where it might.[2] Religious educators must be particularly sensitive when teaching these passages with classical commentary, so that their students do not become superstitious.

DO HUMAN BLESSINGS AND CURSES WORK AUTOMATICALLY?

Isaac's Blessing to Jacob

Isaac's bestowal of the birthright is the central theme of Genesis chapters 25 and 27. Jacob successfully obtains the blessing through deception. Isaac upholds his blessing even after learning that he had mistakenly blessed Jacob:

Isaac was seized with very violent trembling. "Who was it then," he demanded, "that hunted game and brought it to me? Moreover, I ate of it before you came, and I blessed him; now he must remain blessed!" When Esau heard his father's words, he burst into wild and bitter sobbing, and said to his father, "Bless me too, Father!" But he answered, "Your brother came with guile and took away your blessing." [Esau] said, "Was he, then, named Jacob that he might supplant me these two times? First he took away my birthright and now he has taken away my blessing!" (Genesis 27:33-36).

Given his knowledge of Jacob's deception, why does Isaac conclude that "now he must remain blessed" (verse 33)?

Following a Midrash (*Genesis Rabbah* 67:2), Rashi suggests that Isaac said "now he must remain blessed" (verse 33) only *after* hearing that Esau had sold the birthright years earlier (verse 36). Isaac thereby made a rational decision upon learning previously unknown (to Isaac) vital information. Of course, Rashi's interpretation requires reading the verses out of sequence. In the text, Isaac appears to uphold the blessing *immediately* after learning that he was speaking with Esau. Most commentators therefore reject Rashi's reading.

According to Rabbi Joseph Bekhor Shor and Ramban, Isaac's blessing was prophetic and therefore could not be retracted. Ralbag and Abarbanel disagree and suggest that the blessing was not "automatic." Rather, Isaac concluded that since Jacob had deceived him successfully, it must have been God's will that Jacob should be blessed.

To summarize: Rashi, Ralbag, and Abarbanel interpret Isaac's upholding the blessing as Isaac's rational decision. Rabbi Joseph Bekhor Shor and Ramban maintain that Isaac's blessing was an unretractable prophecy. In this latter reading, Isaac was powerless to annul even a misdirected blessing.

Regardless of the aforementioned debate, there is one other critical detail. Although Isaac was unaware (as far as we know), Rebekah received a prophecy during her pregnancy suggesting that Jacob would prevail over Esau:

> The Lord answered her, "Two nations are in your womb, two separate peoples shall issue from your body; one people shall be mightier than the other, and the older shall serve the younger" (Genesis 25:23).

Moreover, several Midrashim and later commentators understand "the older shall serve the younger" (*ve-rav ya'avod tza'ir*) as ambiguous. It could mean "the older shall serve the younger," but it also can mean "the older shall have the younger work for him" (*Genesis Rabbah* 63:7, Radak, Abarbanel). According to the Midrash, God stated the prophecy ambiguously since its favorable fulfillment for Jacob would occur only when Jacob and his descendants are faithful to God and the Torah. In the broader birthright narrative, then, Isaac's human blessing also fulfills God's prophetic plan. Even then, it does not work automatically but appears to be conditional on the future righteous behavior of Jacob and his descendants. According to all of the aforementioned readings, then, Isaac's blessing reflected God's will, and did not invoke some independent power that would bring blessing to Jacob and his descendants regardless.

In this spirit, Malbim (on Genesis 27:1) asserts that Isaac did not have the power to bestow divine blessings of chosenness. Rather, he had power over inheritance. The blessing to be God's nation is solely in God's hands, and that blessing depends on the religious worthiness of Jacob and Esau. Nehama Leibowitz agrees with this approach, and insists that Esau's intermarriage to Canaanites (Genesis 26:34), rather than his sale of the birthright, forfeited his worthiness of the divine blessing. Isaac's blessing of Esau could not have created the third Patriarch of the chosen nation.[3]

Noah's Blessings and Curses

After Ham's shameful behavior toward his drunk and naked father Noah, Shem and Japeth respectfully covered their father. When Noah realized what had happened, he cursed Ham's son Canaan and blessed Shem and Japheth:

> He said, "Cursed be Canaan; the lowest of slaves shall he be to his brothers." And he said, "Blessed be the Lord, the God of Shem; let Canaan be a slave to them. May God enlarge Japheth, and let him dwell in the tents of Shem; and let Canaan be a slave to them" (Genesis 9:25-27).

These blessings are fulfilled when the Canaanites—the descendants of Ham—are dispossessed by the Israelites—the descendants of Shem. Did Noah's blessing and curse cause this critical event in Israel's history?

The answer is negative. God dispossesses the Canaanites because they were wicked (for example, Genesis 15:16; Leviticus 18:24-30; Deuteronomy 9:1-5). The Israelites receive the Land because of God's covenant with the Patriarchs (Deuteronomy 9:1-5). The Israelites also do not retain the Land of Israel automatically. If they are wicked, God will dispossess them from their land as well (for example, Leviticus 26:31-33; Deuteronomy 4:25-28; 11:16-17; 28:64-68). Righteous behavior allows a nation to merit the Land of Israel, and wicked behavior leads God to expel a nation from the Land of Israel.

Like Isaac's blessing to Jacob, then, Noah's blessings and curses reflect the divine will, and play no independent role in the dispossession of the Canaanites nor in God's awarding the Land of Israel to Abraham and his descendants.

Balaam's Blessings and Curses

A similar discussion arises over Balaam's power to curse Israel. The premise of the narrative in Numbers chapters 22-24 is that Balaam's powers were perceived as genuine, and God's intervention on Israel's behalf rescued Israel from the deleterious effects of the curse. Tanakh repeatedly invokes this story to demonstrate God's love of Israel (see Deuteronomy 23:5–6; Joshua 24:9–10; Micah 6:5; Nehemiah 13:1–2).

However, traditional commentators debate the "what if" of the narrative. Had Balaam actually cursed Israel, would Israel have been harmed? Several talmudic passages and later commentators take the premise of the narrative as factual, that is, Balaam indeed would have harmed Israel were it not for God's intervention. However, other commentators maintain that the Moabites and Israelites alike believed in Balaam's powers, but they were objectively mistaken. Balaam could not harm Israel against God's will to bless Israel.[4]

Rachel's Death in Childbirth

Rachel's tragic death as she gave birth to Benjamin is heart-wrenching (Genesis 35:16-20), but the Torah does not explain why she died. Following one Midrash (*Genesis Rabbah* 74:4, 9), Rashi (on Genesis 31:32) ascribes Rachel's death to a curse uttered by Jacob when he proclaimed his innocence in stealing Laban's *terafim* (household idols) several chapters earlier. Jacob did not know that Rachel had stolen the *terafim* and hidden them in her saddle bag (Genesis 31:19, 34-35):

> "But anyone with whom you find your gods shall not remain alive! In the presence of our kinsmen, point out what I have of

yours and take it." Jacob, of course, did not know that Rachel had stolen them (Genesis 31:32).

In this reading, Rachel tragically dies as a result of Jacob's unwitting curse.

However, most commentators do not link Jacob's declaration of innocence to Rachel's death. First, some do not think Jacob's statement is a curse at all, but rather an exaggerated statement that Jacob would kill anyone who stole the idols (Ibn Ezra), or that Laban would have his permission to kill the thief (Radak).

There also is no reason to think that human curses work automatically. When Joseph's brothers emphatically denied stealing Joseph's silver goblet, they stated:

> Whichever of your servants it is found with shall die; the rest
> of us, moreover, shall become slaves to my lord (Genesis 44:9).

Benjamin did not die prematurely as a result of this declaration.

Rejecting Rashi's approach, Ibn Ezra (on Genesis 31:32) observes that childbirth is dangerous. The only other recorded biblical childbirth death is that of the High Priest Eli's son Pinehas' wife (I Samuel 4:19-22). Nobody cursed her, and yet she died. There is no reason to believe from within the text that Jacob's unwitting curse (if it was a curse at all) should be considered a reason for Rachel's death.[5]

DO HEAD COUNTS BRING PLAGUES?

During the commandment to build the Tabernacle, God commands that every Israelite man contribute one half-shekel toward a census:

> When you take a census of the Israelite people according
> to their enrollment, each shall pay the Lord a ransom for

himself on being enrolled, that no plague may come upon them through their being enrolled... the rich shall not pay more and the poor shall not pay less than half a shekel when giving the Lord's offering as expiation for your persons. You shall take the expiation money from the Israelites and assign it to the service of the Tent of Meeting; it shall serve the Israelites as a reminder before the Lord, as expiation for your persons (Exodus 30:12-16).

Regardless of one's means, every man is required to give exactly the prescribed amount "to atone for your lives." The silver from the original census was used to make sockets for the Tabernacle and hooks to connect the boards (Exodus 38:25-28). Every Israelite, rich or poor, thereby contributes equally to this aspect of the Tabernacle.

Why, however, are people threatened with a plague if they do not give a half-shekel?

Rashi submits that counting Israelites by head triggers the "evil eye" and brings a plague. Therefore, they must conduct every census using objects such as half-shekels and then count the objects. Rashi adopts the reading of the talmudic sage Rabbi Eleazar: "Whosoever counts Israel violates a negative precept" (Yoma 22b).[6]

To support his reading, Rashi invokes the narrative of King David's census of Israel in II Samuel 24. Despite Joab's protests, David insisted on counting. The census incurred God's wrath, eliciting a devastating plague that claimed the lives of 70,000 Israelites:

The king said to Joab, his army commander, "Make the rounds of all the tribes of Israel, from Dan to Beer-sheba, and take a census of the people, so that I may know the size of the population." Joab answered the king, "May the Lord your God increase the number of the people a hundredfold, while your own eyes see it! But why should my lord king want this?" However, the king's command to Joab and to the officers of the army remained firm; and Joab and the officers of the army set out, at the instance of the king, to take a census of the people of Israel.... The Lord sent a pestilence upon Israel from morning until the set time; and 70,000 of the people died, from Dan to Beer-sheba (II Samuel 24:2-15).

Rashi asserts that David sinned by not counting with half-shekels or other objects, but instead counted heads.

Ramban (on Numbers 1:2) rejects Rashi's interpretation. Joab opposed the very census, and not its method (of not using half-shekels). There are other legitimate military censuses in Tanakh (see, for example, Numbers 31:4-5; Joshua 8:10; I Samuel 11:8, 13:15, 15:4; II Samuel 18:1). To explain the plague in David's time, Ramban observes that David's is the only military census in Tanakh taken during peace time, rather than at war time. Therefore, the census was unnecessary, displaying arrogance and a lack of trust in God. God plagued Israel as a consequence of a sin in faith, rather than because of the method of the census (see also Ralbag and Rabbi Isaiah of Trani on II Samuel 24).[7]

It appears that Ramban's objection to Rashi is compelling, and there is no connection between the commandment to take half-shekels in Exodus 30 and David's sin in II Samuel chapter 24. How, then, should we understand the threat of a plague in Exodus 30:12?

Rabbi Saadiah Gaon (quoted in Ibn Ezra) submits that the annual half-shekel commanded in Exodus 30 is for support of the Tabernacle and the daily sacrifices. A plague results from laxity in contributing to the building fund and to the nation's sacrifices, and not from conducting a head count. In this approach, there is nothing wrong with counting people by head. There is a problem with people refusing to contribute a minimal amount to participate in the Tabernacle and its service of the nation.

Alternatively, Rabbi Samuel D. Luzzatto (Shadal) maintains that Rashi has the best reading of Exodus 30:12, that there is a threat of a plague for conducting any census without half-shekels. However, the Torah reflects a popular superstitious belief that counting people can lead to a plague, rather than an objective reality.[8] This approach traces back at least as far as Rabbi David Kimhi (1160-1235) and Rabbi Joseph ibn Caspi (1279-1340), who explain several passages in the Torah as reflective of popular superstitions that are not objectively true.[9]

In either reading, the Torah does not teach that head counts elicit divine plagues. Religious sins such as arrogance, lack of faith, and non-participation in the national religious service incur God's wrath.

IS THERE BLACK MAGIC?

The Torah prohibits witchcraft as a capital offense (Exodus 22:17; Leviticus 20:27; Deuteronomy 18:9-13). Our commentators debate whether witchcraft exists, or whether witchcraft does not exist but the Torah prohibits its practice since many pagans believed in its efficacy and used magic in their idolatrous systems. Two biblical narratives bring this question to the fore: The Egyptian magicians in the Torah, and the Witch of Endor in I Samuel chapter 28.

The Egyptian Magicians

Pharaoh's magicians turn their staffs into serpents (Exodus 7:8-13), produce blood (Exodus 7:22), and produce frogs (Exodus 8:3). They are defeated during the plague of lice, which they could not replicate (Exodus 8:14-15), and the plague of boils which kept them from being able to appear before Pharaoh (Exodus 9:11).

In *Sanhedrin* 67b, some sages, followed by Ramban, maintain that black magic exists and that the magicians successfully used it. Other sages in *Sanhedrin* 67b, followed by Abarbanel, assert that there is no magic and the magicians used illusion (*ahizat enayim*). Similarly, some Midrashim (*Exodus Rabbah* 9:10; 10:6) maintain that the magicians used black magic to produce blood and frogs, while others (*Mishnat Rabbi Eliezer* 19, *Midrash ha-Gadol*, quoted in *Torah Shelemah* Exodus 8:7) assert that the magicians cleverly found areas not yet afflicted, invoked their "magic," and then the blood and frogs spread entirely from the divine plague.[10] In this instance, the Torah may be read either way.

The Witch of Endor

Nearing the end of his tragic demise, King Saul turned to a necromanceress out of desperation to ascertain God's will:

> Saul disguised himself; he put on different clothes and set out with two men. They came to the woman by night, and he said, "Please divine for me by a ghost".… At that, the woman asked, "Whom shall I bring up for you?" He answered, "Bring up Samuel for me." Then the woman recognized Samuel, and she shrieked loudly.… "What does he look like?" he asked her. "It is an old man coming up," she said, "and he is wrapped in a robe." Then Saul knew that it was Samuel; and he bowed low in homage with his face to the ground. Samuel said to Saul, "Why have you disturbed me and brought me up?" And Saul answered, "I am in great trouble. The Philistines are attacking me and God has turned away from me; He no longer answers me, either by prophets or in dreams. So I have called you to tell me what I am to do." Samuel said, "Why do you ask

me, seeing that the Lord has turned away from you and has become your adversary? The Lord has done for Himself as He foretold through me: The Lord has torn the kingship out of your hands and has given it to your fellow, to David, because you did not obey the Lord and did not execute His wrath upon the Amalekites. That is why the Lord has done this to you today. Further, the Lord will deliver the Israelites who are with you into the hands of the Philistines. Tomorrow your sons and you will be with me; and the Lord will also deliver the Israelite forces into the hands of the Philistines" (I Samuel 28:8-19).

It appears that the witch successfully conjures up the deceased prophet Samuel's spirit, and the characters saw and heard his spirit. This is the only biblical narrative that reflects a connection between the worlds of the living and the dead.

Radak surveys several rationalist positions which reinterpret the story in light of their belief that witchcraft does not exist. Rabbi Saadiah and Rabbi Hai Gaon maintain that on this singular occasion, *God* miraculously brought Samuel's spirit down. Alternatively, Rabbi Samuel ben Hofni Gaon maintains that the entire episode was fraudulent and Samuel's spirit never appeared. The witch recognized Saul immediately but hid that fact so that she could fool him into thinking that she learned it through her magic. She made an educated guess that Saul would die, since the Philistines were powerful.[11] Ibn Ezra (on Exodus 20:3; Leviticus 19:31) also denies the existence of black magic and maintains that the narrative reflects the mistaken perception of the characters rather than objective reality. Rambam (*Hilkhot Avodah Zarah* 11:16) states more generally that all forms of witchcraft are both forbidden by the Torah and absolute nonsense derived from the pagan world. Only a fool would believe something so patently irrational (see also his discussion in *Guide* 2:46). This debate relates to the broader discussion of how literally traditional interpreters understand biblical texts when confronting conflicts with reason.[12]

Radak (on I Samuel 28:24) rejects the aforementioned readings. The narrative suggests that the witch really conjured up Samuel's spirit, and there is no mention of divine intervention. Ramban (on Exodus 7:11; Leviticus 18:21; Deuteronomy 18:9) also adopts the literal reading of the narrative and agrees that the witch successfully conjured up Samuel's spirit using black magic. These commentators maintain that black magic is prohibited by the Torah, and most of its alleged practitioners are frauds. However, in principle black magic does exist and the Witch of Endor was a true practitioner.

Moshe Garsiel[13] adopts a position similar to Rabbi Saadiah Gaon cited above. The narrative clearly depicts the event as genuine, that is, Samuel's spirit really appeared and communicated a prophetic message to Saul. According to Garsiel (like Rabbi Saadiah Gaon), Tanakh generally portrays witchcraft as fraudulent. In this unique occurrence, however, God miraculously sent Samuel's spirit to communicate with Saul. The witch was shocked herself, and therefore screamed. She also immediately understood that only Saul would merit such a miracle, which is how she knew he was the king: "Then the woman recognized Samuel, and she shrieked loudly, and said to Saul, 'Why have you deceived me? You are Saul!'" (I Samuel 28:12). This revelation was part of God's punishment of Saul, and God specifically refused to answer Saul through legitimate means.[14]

To summarize, the plain sense of the text suggests that Samuel's spirit genuinely appeared to Saul. However, there is no reason to conclude that black magic exists. Rather, this may have been a one-time miraculous occurrence, shocking even the witch herself who was used to deceiving her customers.

CAN ONE DIVINE THE FUTURE WITH SIGNS?

The Torah prohibits divination of the future with signs (Leviticus 19:26). Nevertheless, two biblical narratives present ostensibly righteous figures divining the future with signs and they are successful, suggesting God's providential approval.

Seeking a wife for Isaac, Abraham's servant (midrashically identified as Eliezer, Abraham's servant in Genesis 15:2) prays to God and creates a sign to ascertain God's approval:

And he said, "O Lord, God of my master Abraham, grant me good fortune this day, and deal graciously with my master Abraham: Here I stand by the spring as the daughters of the townsmen come out to draw water; let the maiden to whom I say, 'Please, lower your jar that I may drink,' and who replies, 'Drink, and I will also water your camels'—let her be the one whom You have decreed for Your servant Isaac. Thereby shall I know that You have dealt graciously with my master" (Genesis 24:12-14).

After the servant prayed, Rebekah appeared, drew water for the people and the camels, and clearly was the perfect fit for Isaac. It appears that the servant's divination of the future through this sign receives divine approval in the narrative.

Similarly, King Saul's son Jonathan boldly decides to attack a vast enemy Philistine camp accompanied only by his arms-bearer. He creates a sign that he interprets as signaling divine approval:

Jonathan said, "We'll cross over to those men and let them see us. If they say to us, 'Wait until we get to you,' then we'll stay where we are, and not go up to them. But if they say, 'Come up to us,' then we will go up, for the Lord is delivering them into our hands. That shall be our sign" (I Samuel 14:8-10).

Jonathan goes on to win a spectacular victory and is the hero of the narrative.

Despite their resounding successes, did Abraham's servant and Jonathan violate the Torah's prohibition against divination? Commentators debate the meaning of a talmudic passage:

> Rav himself has said: An omen which is not after the form pronounced by Eliezer, Abraham's servant, or by Jonathan the son of Saul, is not considered a divination (*Hullin* 95b).

Rambam (*Hilkhot Avodah Zarah* 11:4) interprets this passage to mean that the divination of Abraham's servant and Jonathan is forbidden divination.

Raavad of Posquieres sharply rejects Rambam's reading and insists that Abraham's servant and Jonathan were righteous and acted appropriately, as is evident from the narratives. He concludes by saying that if Abraham's servant and Jonathan were alive, they would whip Rambam with fiery lashes. Radak and Ralbag agree with Raavad and maintain that the signs of Abraham's servant and Jonathan were permissible. Rabbi Elhanan Samet explains that Raavad, Radak, and Ralbag interpret the Talmud to mean that unlike the other signs discussed in that passage, which are considered unreliable forms of divination, the signs of Abraham's servant and Jonathan were reliable. The Talmud is giving advice on appropriate divination.[15]

Alternatively, Ran (Rabbenu Nissim on *Hullin* 95b) and Rabbi Joseph Karo (*Kesef Mishneh* on Rambam, *Hilkhot Avodah Zarah* 11:4) agree that the signs of Abraham's servant and Jonathan were appropriate because they are rational. Abraham's servant sought a hospitable wife for Isaac, and Jonathan interpreted the Philistines' summoning him as giving him a military advantage. The Torah prohibits making decisions based on signs that have no rational basis, such as seeing a black cat.

According to Rambam, the Torah outlaws all divination signs, rational or not. For the others, Abraham's servant and Jonathan sought signs of divine providence using rational means and prayer. The plain sense of the narratives supports the majority opinion against Rambam, that Abraham's servant and Jonathan acted appropriately and were blessed with divine assistance.[16]

CONCLUSION

The plain sense of the biblical texts we have considered does not support the notion that human blessings or curses work automatically without divine support. There also is no evidence that a head count automatically elicits a plague. The plain sense of the narrative in I Samuel 28 (and possibly also the Egyptian magicians) might suggest the existence of black magic, but a number of commentators exclude that possibility and provide a fair alternative reading of the text. Regardless, the Torah outlaws sorcery as a capital offense. It appears from the plain sense of the text that the signs of Abraham's servant and Jonathan are acceptable in the context of faith in God and rationality. Rambam rules otherwise, and prohibits all forms of divination.

While some Midrashim and later commentators ascribe some of these events to automatically triggered forces, it appears that Tanakh indeed attempts to eradicate superstitions at their roots. God rules the entire universe, and people's righteous or wicked behavior, not magic, determines God's providential relationship with humanity.

A final note to educators: While Rashi often is the exclusive commentator taught to children throughout much of elementary school, educators of young children should give serious pause before teaching Rashi's comments about the issues discussed in this essay. Since it is difficult to present complex and conflicting views on these subjects to young children, elementary school students will necessarily adopt the view that Rachel died because of Jacob's unwitting curse and that head counts invoke the "evil eye." It is preferable to defer these discussions at least until high school, when children are old enough to learn the different sides of these debates.

NOTES

1. For further discussion, see, for example, Nahum M. Sarna, "Paganism and Biblical Judaism," in *Studies in Biblical Interpretation* (Philadelphia: Jewish Publication Society, 2000), pp. 13-28; Christine Hayes, *Introduction to the Bible* (New Haven: Yale University Press, 2012), pp. 15-28.

2. A different, and much broader, discussion pertains to rabbinic statements in the Talmud and mystical literature and later rabbinic interpretations, particularly that of Rambam. See, for example, Menachem Kellner, *Maimonides' Confrontation with Mysticism* (Oxford: The Littman Library of Jewish Civilization, 2006); Marc B. Shapiro, *Studies in Maimonides and His Interpreters* (Scranton: University of Scranton Press, 2008), pp. 95-150; H. Norman Strickman, *Without Red Strings or Holy Water: Maimonides' Mishneh Torah* (Boston: Academic Studies Press, 2011).

3. Nehama Leibowitz, *Studies in Bereshit (Genesis)*, trans. Aryeh Newman (Jerusalem: Eliner Library), pp. 277-278.

4. For a survey of traditional opinions, see Yehuda Nachshoni, *Studies in the Weekly Parashah: Bamidbar*, trans. Raphael Blumberg and Yaakov Petroff (Jerusalem: Mesorah Publications, 1989), pp. 1091–1098.

5. See further sources and discussion in Elhanan Samet, *Iyyunim be-Parashot ha-Shavua* (second series) vol. 1 (Hebrew) ed. Ayal Fishler (Ma'aleh Adumim: Ma'aliyot Press, 2004), pp. 156-160.

6. Rashi also follows Rabbi Elazar (Yoma 22b) on I Samuel 15:4, when King Saul counted his troops prior to his battle against Amalek: "Saul mustered the troops and enrolled them at Telaim [*va-yifkedem ba-tela'im*]: 200,000 men on foot, and 10,000 men of Judah." Rashi interprets *va-yifkedem ba-tela'im* to mean that he counted them using sheep, rather than counting them by head. Radak disagrees and interprets "Tela'im" as the name of a place (the NJPS translation cited in this note adopts this reading). In Radak's reading, Saul did not specifically use objects, but simply counted his troops.

7. In I Chronicles, there is a brief note of a related problem, that of counting all of Israel. God promised that Israel would be as numerous as the stars, and therefore a census is limiting: "David did not take a census

of those under twenty years of age, for the Lord had promised to make Israel as numerous as the stars of heaven. Joab son of Zeruiah did begin to count them, but he did not finish; wrath struck Israel on account of this, and the census was not entered into the account of the chronicles of King David" (I Chronicles 27:23-24). From this vantage point, counting all of Israel, with or without half-shekels, remains the problem. However, military censuses are appropriate under normal circumstances.

8. See further discussion in Moshe Shamah, *Recalling the Covenant: A Contemporary Commentary on the Five Books of the Torah* (Jersey City, NJ: Ktav, 2011), pp. 445-460.

9. See Jerome Yehuda Gellman, *This Was from God: A Contemporary Theology of Torah and History* (Boston: Academic Studies Press, 2016), pp. 122-123.

10. Nahum M. Sarna observes that there is an Egyptian species of cobra rendered rigid by applying pressure to a nerve at the nape of its neck. When thrown to the ground, the jolt causes it to recover and it wriggles away (*Exploring Exodus: The Origins of Biblical Israel* [New York: Schocken, 1986–1996], pp. 67-68).

11. In this reading, how could the witch have known that Saul was rejected by God? Samuel's prophecy was not public knowledge.

12. See Hayyim Angel, "Controversies over the Historicity of Biblical Passages in Traditional Commentary," in Angel, *The Keys to the Palace: Essays Exploring the Religious Value of Reading the Bible* (New York: Kodesh Press, 2017), pp. 115-131.

13. Moshe Garsiel, *Reshit ha-Melukhah BeYisrael*, vol. 2 (Hebrew), (Raananah: Open University Press, 2008), pp. 302-303.

14. For a fuller discussion of rabbinic and Karaite views of the tenth-twelfth centuries and their influences, see Haggai ben Shammai, "From Rabbinic Homilies to Geonic Doctrinal Exegesis: The Story of the Witch of En Dor as a Test Case," in *Exegetical Crossroads: Understanding Scripture in Judaism, Christianity and Islam in the Pre-Modern Orient*, ed. Georges Tamer et al. (Berlin: De Gruyter, 2018), pp. 163-197.

15. Elhanan Samet, *Iyyunim be-Parashot ha-Shavua* (second series) vol. 2 (Hebrew) ed. Ayal Fishler (Ma'aleh Adumim: Ma'aliyot Press, 2004),

pp. 389-407. An English version can be found at http://etzion.org.il/en/ prohibition-divination-rambam-vs-sages-provence, accessed June 26, 2018.

16. Jacob Milgrom adopts a similar perspective. Sorcery is when one tries to alter the future with magic. This practice is absolutely incompatible with monotheism and is a capital crime in the Torah since a magician tries to overrule God's will. In contrast, divination is when one tries to predict the future using signs. This practice *could* be compatible with monotheism if one claims to predict the future God intends. Milgrom appeals to Abraham's servant and Jonathan as examples that can be tolerated (*Anchor Bible: Leviticus 17-22* [New York: Doubleday, 2000], pp. 1687-1688). Milgrom disagrees with Yehezkel Kaufmann, who maintained (like Rambam) that divination is incompatible with biblical monotheism.

LOVE THE GER:
A BIBLICAL PERSPECTIVE*

INTRODUCTION

In this essay, we will step back into the biblical world, and explore the Torah's attitude toward the *ger*. Before proceeding, we must understand that in the Oral Law, there are two categories of *gerim*: what we call a convert today is the *ger tzedek*, "righteous convert," who becomes a permanent member of the Jewish people. There also is a category of *ger toshav*, "resident alien." These are non-Jewish individuals who live in Israel and adopt certain standards of belief and practice (to be discussed below), but do not become Jewish through a formal process of conversion.

The plain sense of the Torah does not have these two categories. Rather, a *ger* always is a resident alien, and refers to non-Israelites who permanently live in Israel. The biblical term *ger* more broadly refers to people living in a land that does not belong to them (see Rashi on Exodus 22:20). God tells Abraham that his descendants will be *gerim* in a land that is not theirs (Genesis 15:13).[1] Abraham refers to himself as a *ger ve-toshav* to the Hittites when he attempts to purchase a burial site for Sarah (Genesis 23:4).[2] Israelites even have the status of *gerim ve-toshavim* in their own land, since it belongs to God (Leviticus 25:23).[3] When the Israelites lived in Egypt, the idea that they were *gerim* has nothing to do with converting to Egyptian religion. The same conversely applies to *gerim* living in Israel—they do not adopt Israelite religion, but live permanently in the land.[4]

---

* This essay is forthcoming in *Conversations* 36 (Autumn 2020).

When the Written Law differs from the Oral Law, we apply the Oral Law in practice, but the Written Law still teaches central values of the Torah. This article focuses on the respective values taught by the Written and Oral Law.

THE *GER* IN THE TORAH

The Torah assumes that most *gerim* require the support of the community, and it regularly lists them among the vulnerable members of society.[5] *Gerim* were not landowners (women like Ruth had an easier time integrating into Israelite society, since they could marry Israelite landowners), and often had no family network nearby for support.[6] The Torah exhorts Israel to care for *gerim* and to love them. God loves them, and Israel should love them and have compassion on them since the Israelites were *gerim* themselves in Egypt:

> When a stranger resides with you in your land, you shall not wrong him. The stranger who resides with you shall be to you as one of your citizens; you shall love him as yourself, for you were strangers [*gerim*] in the land of Egypt: I the Lord am your God (Leviticus 19:33-34).

> For the Lord your God is God supreme and Lord supreme, the great, the mighty, and the awesome God, who shows no favor and takes no bribe, but upholds the cause of the fatherless and the widow, and befriends the stranger, providing him with food and clothing. You too must befriend the stranger, for you were strangers [*gerim*] in the land of Egypt (Deuteronomy 10:17-19).

> The Talmud (*Bava Metzia* 59b) counts 36 references to treating the *ger* fairly, making it one of the most frequently reiterated commandments of the Torah.[7]

Civil law treats Israelites and *gerim* equally (Leviticus 24:22).[8] Strikingly, the Torah also obligates the *ger* to observe many ritual commandments. For example:

- *Gerim* may not eat leaven (*hametz*) on Passover (Exodus 12:19).
- *Gerim* may not do work on Shabbat (Exodus 20:10; Deuteronomy 5:13; cf. Exodus 23:12).
- *Gerim* may not do work on Yom Kippur (Leviticus 16:29).
- *Gerim* may not eat blood (Leviticus 17:10-13).
- *Gerim* must refrain from all prohibited sexual relationships and Molech worship (Leviticus 18:26).
- *Gerim* may bring sacrifices in the Tabernacle (Numbers 15:14-16).
- *Gerim* incur the severe punishment of *karet* (excision) if they commit severe intentional sins (Numbers 15:29-31).
- *Gerim* must attend the public Torah reading (*hakhel*) every seven years (Deuteronomy 31:12). This law is similar to the acceptance of the covenant in Deuteronomy 29:10, which includes the *ger*.

There are exceptions which exempt *gerim* from certain laws binding on Israelites:

- *Gerim* may eat carrion (*nevelah*) (Deuteronomy 14:21).
- *Gerim* may become permanent slaves, unlike Israelites, who must go free at the Jubilee year (Leviticus 25:45-46).

The laws of the Passover sacrifice similarly suggest differences between Israelites and *gerim*:

If a stranger who dwells with you would offer the Passover to the Lord, all his males must be circumcised; then he shall be admitted to offer it; he shall then be as a citizen of the country. But no uncircumcised person may eat of it. There shall be one law for the citizen and for the stranger who dwells among you (Exodus 12:48-49).

Ibn Ezra explains that *gerim* are not required to bring the Passover sacrifice. However, those who wish to may do so, if they first circumcise their males.[9] This law also implies that *gerim* are not required to be circumcised unless they choose to participate in the Passover sacrifice.[10]

The commandment to dwell in booths on Sukkot applies to Israelite citizens (*ezrah*) without reference to the *ger*:

You shall live in booths seven days; all citizens in Israel shall live in booths, in order that future generations may know that I made the Israelite people live in booths when I brought them out of the land of Egypt, I the Lord your God (Leviticus 23:42-43).

Rashbam explains that Israelite citizens must remember their humble origins as a nation in the desert so they do not become arrogant with their homes and wealth in Israel. This reasoning does not apply to *gerim*.[11]

THE ORAL LAW

The Oral Law redefines the meaning of *ger* in the Torah by applying the two concepts of *ger tzedek* and *ger toshav*. Any equations of *ezrah* and *ger* in the Torah are understood in the Oral Law as referring exclusively to the *ger tzedek*. Therefore, a *ger toshav* is not obligated to observe the Torah's commandments directed at the *ger*.

The commandment to love *gerim* likewise is understood in the Oral Law as referring exclusively to the *ger tzedek*, and not to the *ger toshav*. The gap between the *peshat* of the Torah and the Oral Law is particularly conspicuous in Leviticus, where we find separate commandments to love one's neighbor and *gerim*:

> You shall not take vengeance or bear a grudge against your countrymen. Love your fellow as yourself: I am the Lord (Leviticus 19:18).

> The stranger who resides with you shall be to you as one of your citizens; you shall love him as yourself, for you were strangers in the land of Egypt: I the Lord am your God (Leviticus 19:34).

The plain sense of the text appears to refer to two groups of people. "Neighbor" (*re'a*) likely refers to fellow Israelites (*Sifra Kedoshim* 8:4, *Mishnat Rabbi Eliezer* 16),[12] whereas the "stranger" (*ger*) likely refers to the *ger toshav*, resident alien. However, the Oral Law understands the law of loving the stranger to refer to the righteous convert, the *ger tzedek*. Wouldn't that commandment already be included under the commandment to love one's neighbor? Rambam (*Hilkhot De'ot* 6:4) explains that there is a double-commandment to love converts. We must love them as we love any fellow Jew, and we also have an additional commandment to love converts.

To summarize: There are two fundamental discrepancies between the *peshat* understanding of the Torah's use of *ger* (which always refers to the *ger toshav*) and the Oral Law (which almost always understands the *ger* in the Torah as a *ger tzedek*): (1) Proper treatment: We must love, care for, and not oppress the *ger*. All of these commandments refer exclusively to the righteous convert and not the resident alien. (2) The *ger* obligated to observe commandments like Israelite citizens is the righteous convert, and not the resident alien. The *ger tzedek* is a fully naturalized Jew who enjoys both the protections and obligations of being part of the Jewish people in his or her covenant with the God of Israel.

There is one verse that the Oral Law must interpret as referring to the *ger toshav*:

> You shall not eat anything that has died a natural death; give it to the stranger (*ger*) in your community to eat, or you may sell it to a foreigner. For you are a people consecrated to the Lord your God. You shall not boil a kid in its mother's milk (Deuteronomy 14:21).

Since Israelites are prohibited from eating carrion (*nevelah*), righteous converts obviously are prohibited, as well. Therefore, this *ger* must be a *ger toshav*.[13]

By interpreting most Torah references to *gerim* as denoting the *ger tzedek*, there is little left for the Oral Law to define the Torah's requirements of a *ger toshav*. They are permitted to eat carrion, but what obligations or restrictions do they have?

A talmudic debate supplies a range of views, from minimalist to maximalist (*Avodah Zarah* 64b). Some suggest that if carrion is permitted, most other Torah laws likewise are not applicable to the *ger toshav*. One Sage rules that the *ger toshav* must refrain from idolatry. Others maintain that they must observe the Seven Noahide Laws so they are ethical monotheists.[14] Leviticus 18:28 supports this position, stating that the Canaanites forfeited their right to live in the Land of Israel because of their sexual immorality and Molech worship, which includes child sacrifice (which violates the prohibition of both idolatry and murder): "So let not the land spew you out for defiling it, as it spewed out the nation that came before you."[15]

A third view in the Talmud suggests that the *ger toshav* is permitted carrion, but is obligated by all other laws of the Torah. This view is much closer to the *peshat* of the Torah, which indeed applies many laws equally to Israelite citizens and the *ger*, i.e., the *ger toshav*.

EXPLAINING THE GAP BETWEEN
THE WRITTEN AND ORAL LAW

In his analysis of this topic, Rabbi Yehuda Rock[16] observes that there are two competing values within the Torah for the one category of *ger toshav*: (1) There is a goal of the unification of everyone living in the land of Israel under God and the Torah, so there is one equal law for everyone. (2) Israel is a holy nation and has a unique relationship with God. The permission for a *ger toshav* to eat carrion in Deuteronomy 14:21 is stated in the context of Israel's special holiness, "for you are a people consecrated to the Lord your God."

We may add to Rabbi Rock's analysis by reviewing the other explicit distinctions between the Israelite citizen and the *ger* in the Torah. In Ibn Ezra's reading of Exodus 12:48 cited above, *gerim* are not obligated in the Passover Sacrifice (nor in circumcision), but those who wish to participate must circumcise their males. Both of these commandments are unique covenantal laws that govern the God-Israel relationship and do not pertain to the *ger*.

The same applies to the reason Israelites cannot have permanent slavery (Leviticus 25:45-46). Through their singular covenantal relationship with God, they are God's servants and cannot be slaves of humans forever.

Finally, the Torah singles out an obligation for Israelites to dwell in booths on Sukkot (Leviticus 23:42-43), since they alone have the historical narrative of the sojourn in the wilderness.

To summarize: In general, all who live in Israel must observe the laws of the land, be cared for and loved, and receive equal treatment. In covenantal laws that highlight the unique God-Israel relationship, the *ger* is exempt and distinguished from Israelite citizens.

The Oral Law distinguishes between the *ger tzedek* who is bound by *all* of the Torah's laws and is loved and cared for by Israelites, and the *ger toshav* who must accept certain minimal standards to live in Israel. Since the Oral Law understands the commandments to love the *ger* as referring exclusively to the *ger tzedek*, it concludes that regarding the *ger toshav*, "you are obligated to sustain him" (*Pesahim* 21b).[17]

CONCLUSION

The Oral Law teaches that a core Jewish value is to love converts to Judaism. The Written Law teaches that same love and inclusion of the resident alien, complete with rights and responsibilities. The Torah teaches a remarkable love, sensitivity, and fair treatment of all people living in the Land of Israel.

The Torah commands the *ger* to participate in the *hakhel* ceremony every seven years, to participate in the acceptance of the Torah (Deuteronomy 31:12). In this spirit, Joshua executes a public Torah acceptance after crossing into the Land of Israel, and there are *gerim* present:

> All Israel—stranger and citizen alike—with their elders, officials, and magistrates, stood on either side of the Ark.... There was not a word of all that Moses had commanded that Joshua failed to read in the presence of the entire assembly of Israel, including the women and children and the strangers who accompanied them (Joshua 8:33-35).

That God-fearing non-Israelites may serve God in the Temple traces its roots to Numbers 15:14-16:

> And when, throughout the ages, a stranger who has taken up residence with you, or one who lives among you, would present an offering by fire of pleasing odor to the Lord—as you do, so shall it be done by the rest of the congregation. There shall be one law for you and for the resident stranger; it shall be a law for all time throughout the ages. You and the stranger shall be alike before the Lord; the same ritual and the same rule shall apply to you and to the stranger who resides among you.

King Solomon proclaimed this welcome message at the dedication of the First Temple:

> Or if a foreigner who is not of Your people Israel comes from a distant land for the sake of Your name—for they shall hear about Your great name and Your mighty hand and Your outstretched arm—when he comes to pray toward this House, oh, hear in Your heavenly abode and grant all that the foreigner asks You for. Thus all the peoples of the earth will know Your name and revere You, as does Your people Israel; and they will recognize that Your name is attached to this House that I have built (I Kings 8:41-43).

This ideal carries over into the exalted messianic visions in the Book of Isaiah:

> In the days to come, the Mount of the Lord's House shall stand firm above the mountains and tower above the hills; and all the nations shall gaze on it with joy. And the many peoples shall go and say: "Come, let us go up to the Mount

of the Lord, to the House of the God of Jacob; that He may instruct us in His ways, and that we may walk in His paths." For instruction shall come forth from Zion, the word of the Lord from Jerusalem (Isaiah 2:2-3).

As for the foreigners who attach themselves to the Lord, to minister to Him, and to love the name of the Lord, to be His servants—all who keep the Sabbath and do not profane it, and who hold fast to My covenant—I will bring them to My sacred mount and let them rejoice in My house of prayer. Their burnt offerings and sacrifices shall be welcome on My altar; for My House shall be called a house of prayer for all peoples (Isaiah 56:6-7).

In a novel extension of these values, Ezekiel prophesies that in the ideal future, *gerim* even will own land in Israel:

You shall allot it as a heritage for yourselves and for the strangers who reside among you, who have begotten children among you. You shall treat them as Israelite citizens; they shall receive allotments along with you among the tribes of Israel. You shall give the stranger an allotment within the tribe where he resides—declares the Lord God (Ezekiel 47:22-23).

One cannot envision greater integration of the *ger* than this.[18]

NOTES

1. This term is used regularly throughout the Torah in reference to Israel's sojourn in Egypt. See Exodus 22:20; 23:9; Leviticus 19:33-34; Deuteronomy 10:19; 23:8; 24:17-22.

2. See also Exodus 2:22, referring to Zipporah's birth of Moses' son Gershom: "She bore a son whom he named Gershom, for he said, 'I have been a stranger in a foreign land.'" Cf. Exodus 18:3.

3. See also Psalm 39:13; I Chronicles 29:15.

4. A different term, *nokhri*, tends to refer to non-Israelites who come to Israel on a temporary basis, such as merchants.

5. See, for example, Leviticus 19:10; 23:22; 25:6; Deuteronomy 14:29; 16:11, 14; 24:17; 26:11; 27:19.

6. The Torah acknowledges the possibility that some *gerim* will become wealthy (Leviticus 25:47), and it is a curse if Israelites sin and decline while the *ger* rises (Deuteronomy 28:43).

7. Nehama Leibowitz went so far as to suggest that the *reason* God wanted the Israelites to be enslaved in Egypt was so that they would develop a sensitivity toward the underprivileged (*New Studies in Shemot-Exodus*, pp. 1-11).

8. See also Numbers 35:15; Deuteronomy 24:17; 27:19.

9. They also must be in a state of ritual purity like any Israelite (see Numbers 9:6-7, 13-14).

10. The Oral Law interprets this passage as referring to the *ger tzedek*, the righteous convert. It therefore understands the verse as requiring the *ger* to bring the Passover sacrifice (Rambam, *Hilkhot Korban Pesah* 9:7).

11. Jacob Milgrom (*Anchor Bible: Leviticus 17-22* [New York: Doubleday, 2000], pp. 1496-1499) maintains that the *ger* must refrain from prohibitions since violation of negative commandments pollutes the land, whereas the *ger* is exempt from positive commandments. Milgrom explains the anomalous permission for the *ger* to eat carrion in Deuteronomy 14:21 as a means of preserving some distinction between Israelites and *gerim*. This explanation, however, is unconvincing, given the Torah's equation of Israelites and *gerim* in every other arena.

12. For a survey of Jewish views through the ages, with emphasis on a sea change in interpretation toward viewing "Love your neighbor" as a reference to all humanity in more recent times, see Reinhard Neudecker ("'And You Shall Love Your Neighbor as Yourself—I Am the Lord' (Lev 19,18) in Jewish Interpretation," *Biblica* 73 (1992), pp. 496-517. See also the illuminating moral debate between Ernst Simon, "The Neighbor (*Re'a*) Whom We Shall Love," and the response of Harold Fisch, in *Modern Jewish Ethics: Theory and Practice*, ed. Marvin Fox (Ohio: Ohio State University Press, 1975), pp. 29-61.

13. The Septuagint reflects the same distinction. Jacob Milgrom notes, "[T]he Septuagint [invented] a new word, *proselutos* 'proselyte,' for the convert, a term they consistently use for *ger* in all legal contexts. The sole exception is Exod 12:19, where they use the transliterated (Aramaic) form *geioras*, and Deut 14:21, where, in order to prevent concluding that the convert may eat of a *nebela*, they translate *ger* as *paroikos* 'alien' (*Anchor Bible: Leviticus 17-22*, p. 1501).

14. Rambam (*Hilkhot Issurei Bi'ah* 14:7-8) rules that the *ger toshav* must renounce idolatry and commit to observe the Seven Noahide Laws. Rambam rules further that the laws of *ger toshav* are inapplicable today, since *halakhah* links those laws to the laws of the Jubilee Year. Rabbi Saul Zucker (unpublished essay, emailed to author May 5, 2020) explains that the *ger toshav* accepts a connection to Israel as a nation, in contrast to the *ger tzedek* who accepts a connection to Israel's religion. Therefore, a halakhic *ger toshav* does not exist at a time when Israel is insufficiently constituted in its land to observe the Jubilee year. I am grateful to Rabbi Zucker for sharing his piece with me.

15. See also Deuteronomy 12:31; 18:9-12.

16. Yehuda Rock, "Love for the *Ger*," at https://www.etzion.org.il/en/love-ger. Accessed April 24, 2020.

17. Yehuda Rock analyzes that talmudic law. Here are his words (see reference in previous note), with minor modifications:

> The substance of this requirement is a matter of debate among the Rishonim (medieval rabbinic authorities). According to Ramban (*Gloss to Sefer Ha-mitzvot*, Positive 16; *Commentary*, Leviticus 25:35),

it refers to saving his life…. Rambam views this requirement as the provision of support—i.e., communal responsibility that facilitates the conduct of life, including also basic manners and acts of kindness (*Hilkhot Melakhim* 10:12). The Gemara does not state explicitly the source for this command "to sustain him," but the Rishonim (Rashi, ad loc; Rambam, *Hilkhot Zekhiyya* 3:11; Ramban, ibid.) point to Leviticus 25:35: "If your brother grows poor, and his means fail with you, you shall support him—a stranger (*ger*) or a resident (*toshav*)—that he may survive with you." The structure of this verse is somewhat opaque, but the message seems to be that the command to support and sustain a brother extends to include a "*ger or toshav*." The Sages explain (*Torat Kohanim*, ad loc), "'Ger' – this means a *ger tzedek*; 'toshav' – this means a *ger* who eats carcasses." In other words, the *ger* mentioned in the verse is a convert, as the word is usually used by the Sages; the *toshav* mentioned in the verse is actually a *ger toshav*. This, then, is the source of the requirement to support and sustain even a *ger toshav*.

18. *Sifri Beha'alotekha* 78 reinterprets Ezekiel to refer to atonement rather than land inheritance. Several classical commentators interpret the passage as referring to the *ger tzedek* who will inherit land (see, e.g., Rashi, Radak, Abarbanel, Malbim).

AMOS

PROPHETIC EMPHASIS ON ETHICS[*]

HISTORICAL BACKGROUND[1]

Amos prophesied during the reign of Uzziah (788-736 BCE). Uzziah reigned in the Southern Kingdom while Jeroboam II ruled the Northern Kingdom (789-748 BCE). Jeroboam II reigned 41 years, the longest ever for a Northern monarch; and Uzziah reigned 52 years, the longest ever to that point for a Southern monarch (II Kings 15:1-7). The Book of Kings reports little about their lengthy reigns, except that there was strength and prosperity (see II Kings 14:23-29).

The success of this period has prompted scholars to refer to it as a biblical "silver age," second only to the golden age of David and Solomon. Tragically, many Israelites adopted a hedonistic, immoral lifestyle as a consequence of their newfound wealth and political power. They lived such opulent lifestyles that they sold poor Israelites into slavery and engaged in other forms of corruption to meet their outrageous expenses. Their behavior earned them the fierce condemnation of Amos.

Amos stressed that fear of God and ethical conduct were the keys to building an enduring future. Unfortunately, most people failed to heed him, leading to devastating natural disasters and then Assyrian invasions that resulted in the exile of the Northern Kingdom.

---

[*] This essay appeared originally in *Conversations* 31 (Spring 2018), pp. 19-26.

ETHICAL CONDUCT DIRECTLY
AFFECTS ISRAEL'S NATIONAL FATE

The Torah equates service of God and moral behavior as all divinely commanded and of absolute importance. However, the Torah and the historical prophetic books referred to as the "Early Prophets" (Joshua, Judges, Samuel, and Kings) focus almost exclusively on faithfulness to God when it comes to determining the fate of the people of Israel as a nation.

The Golden Calf, the sin of the spies, and other Torah narratives about Israel's wrongdoings revolve around Israel's unfaithfulness to God. God also threatens national exile for idolatry (and violation of the sabbatical year) when specific sins are mentioned as opposed to general evil (Leviticus 26; Deuteronomy 4:25-28; 6:14-15; 7:1-5; 8:19-20; 11:16-17; 28:14, 20, 47, 58). Following the Torah's lead, the books of the "Early Prophets" ascribe national punishments and exile to idolatry and unfaithfulness, even as they treat moral sins with great seriousness as well.

Amos' great innovation on the biblical landscape is that Israel's moral state directly affects its national destiny. Arguably, the Book of Amos is *exclusively* about morality. Despite the fact that Israel certainly had problems with idolatry in his time, Amos never explicitly condemns it nor any other sin pertaining to Israel's direct service of God. Instead, Amos excoriates Israel for serving God through sacrifice and other ritual observances, while maintaining an immoral lifestyle.

In contrast, Amos' contemporary Hosea focuses primarily on Israel's unfaithfulness to God because of their idolatry and related sins. Hosea's message is far more consistent with the message of the Torah and the "Early Prophets," that betrayal of God—generally through idolatry—leads to exile.

Amos' central message may be summarized as follows: The Northern Kingdom of Israel has acted wickedly like the people of Sodom. Therefore, it will be devastated like Sodom via an earthquake,[2] other natural disasters, and the Assyrian invasion and exile.[3] Only at the very end of the book does Amos deviate from God's harsh judgment and provide a glimpse of God's love of Israel. The righteous remnant of Israel will endure forever and be redeemed in the future (9:8-15).

PROPHECIES AGAINST THE NATIONS:
GOD HATES IMMORALITY

The Book of Amos opens with prophecies against seven nations (1:3-2:5). Each nation has sinned unforgivably, and now will bear God's wrath, expressed through the upcoming Assyrian invasion that will ravage the entire region. The sins of the six non-Israelite nations are immoral crimes. The sin of Judah—the seventh nation on this roster—is general unfaithfulness against God and the Torah.

Regarding the six non-Israelite nations, it is initially unclear if God punishes them because they are immoral, or because they are immoral *against Israel* and God loves Israel. For example, Amos' first prophecy is against Aram:

Thus said the Lord: For three transgressions of Damascus, for four, I will not revoke it: Because they threshed Gilead with threshing boards of iron. I will send down fire upon the palace of Hazael, and it shall devour the fortresses of Ben-hadad. I will break the gate bars of Damascus, and wipe out the inhabitants from the Vale of Aven and the sceptered ruler of Beth-eden; and the people of Aram shall be exiled to Kir—said the Lord (1:3-5).

107

The sins of the Philistines, Tyre, Edom, and Ammon follow the same pattern. These nations harmed Israel, so God will punish them.[4]

The prophecy against Moab—the sixth nation on the list—becomes a litmus test for interpreters, since it refers to Moab's immoral treatment of Edom, and not Israel:

> Thus said the Lord: For three transgressions of Moab, for four, I will not revoke it: Because he burned the bones of the king of Edom to lime. I will send down fire upon Moab, and it shall devour the fortresses of Kerioth. And Moab shall die in tumult, amid shouting and the blare of horns; I will wipe out the ruler from within her and slay all her officials along with him—said the Lord (2:1-3).

Based on the first five prophecies, which pertain to nations' harming Israel, several commentators conclude that Amos' prophecies against the nations reflect God's love of Israel. Consequently, they interpret Amos' prophecy against Moab in this particularistic spirit. For example, Ibn Ezra observes that Edom descends from Esau, the son of Isaac. Therefore, he maintains that the six prophecies against the nations reflect God's avenging immoral sins against the descendants of Isaac. Alternatively, Radak, Abarbanel, and several other interpreters attempt to connect Amos' prophecy to a narrative in II Kings 3:27, which (in their reading) might suggest that Moab's wronging Edom also brought harm onto Israel.

However, Rashi appears to have the most likely reading. God is outraged by all human immorality, whether or not it is directed against Israel. This universalistic message best encapsulates Amos' prophecies against the nations, and his entire book. For that matter, this message is consistent with narratives in the Torah such as God's punishing Cain for murdering Abel, bringing the Flood, and destroying Sodom, events that have nothing to do with the people of Israel.

PROPHECY AGAINST ISRAEL:
ISRAEL MUST ACT MORALLY

No other prophetic book begins with a prediction of the downfall of other nations. Most prophetic books position their prophecies against the nations after prophecies to Israel. In his *Da'at Mikra* commentary, Amos Hakham suggests that Amos may have begun his prophecy with the downfall of other nations to catch the attention of his audience and gain him support. Israel would be happy to hear of the impending doom of their surrounding enemies. Amos then would be able to shock his audience with the climactic prophecy against the Northern Kingdom[5]:

> Thus said the Lord: For three transgressions of Israel, for four, I will not revoke it: because they have sold for silver those whose cause was just, and the needy for a pair of sandals. [Ah,] you who trample the heads of the poor into the dust of the ground, and make the humble walk a twisted course! Father and son go to the same girl, and thereby profane My holy name. They recline by every altar on garments taken in pledge, and drink in the House of their God wine bought with fines they imposed (2:6-8).

The Northern Kingdom of Israel is the only group mentioned in Amos' diatribe whose members inflict harm on fellow members of their nation. All the other nations' crimes involve their harming people from other nations. It is significant that Amos enumerates only ethical sins for Israel. Although Amos refers to worship at shrines, his intent appears to be that the Israelites think they are righteous by serving God through their religious rituals. God responds that these rituals are worthless and hypocritical when unaccompanied by ethical behavior (Amos Hakham).[6]

The theme of Israel's hiding their immorality behind the observance of religious rituals to God finds its fullest and clearest expression later in the book:

> I loathe, I spurn your festivals, I am not appeased by your solemn assemblies. If you offer Me burnt offerings—or your meal offerings—I will not accept them; I will pay no heed to your gifts of fatlings. Spare Me the sound of your hymns, and let Me not hear the music of your lutes. But let justice well up like water, righteousness like an unfailing stream (5:21-24).

Prophets regularly stress that God does not need sacrifices and other religious rituals. They are acceptable to God only when accompanied by righteous moral behavior. Sacrifices and other acts of worship are essential aspects of Israel's relationship with God, but immorality undermines the very validity of these acts of worship.[7]

Amos regularly attempted to debunk widespread misconceptions among the populace. Wealthy Israelites wrongly believed that their wealth and military power demonstrated divine favor (see, for example, 6:4-6, 13). To counter these misguided attitudes, Amos links poverty and righteousness by referring to poor people as righteous and humble (2:6-7).[8] While of course in reality some poor people could be wicked and some rich people could be righteous, Amos used this extreme formulation to refute the people's dangerous theology.

THE CHOSEN PEOPLE:
ADDITIONAL MORAL RESPONSIBILITY

Amos also deflated the people's wrongful perception of the concept of the "Chosen People."[9] The people believed that since God chose Israel, they were free to do whatever they wanted. Amos countered that God's unique relationship with Israel implies that Israel has an even greater moral responsibility than other nations (Rabbi Joseph Kara, Ibn Ezra, Radak):

> Hear this word, O people of Israel, that the Lord has spoken concerning you, concerning the whole family that I brought up from the land of Egypt: You alone have I singled out of all the families of the earth—that is why I will call you to account for all your iniquities (3:1-2).

The Israelites' confidence in their chosenness also led them to misunderstand the concept of "the day of God," when God metes out judgment against wicked people. The Israelites believed that the day of God would benefit Israel, as it would signal God's defeat of Israel's enemies. Amos shatters this misconception, insisting that wicked Israel is vulnerable to the same judgment on the "day of God" that other wicked people are (Malbim, Amos Hakham[10]):

> Ah, you who wish for the day of the Lord! Why should you want the day of the Lord? It shall be darkness, not light!—As if a man should run from a lion and be attacked by a bear; or if he got indoors, should lean his hand on the wall and be bitten by a snake! Surely the day of the Lord shall be not light, but darkness, blackest night without a glimmer (5:18-20).

This prophecy relates back to the prophecies against other nations at the beginning of the book, which reaches its climax with

Amos' prophecy against Israel. This idea was shocking to the popular conception of religion, which imagined God smiting Israel's enemies and then redeeming Israel regardless of Israel's religious conduct.

The book's conclusion presents one of the starkest pictures of Israel's chosenness in the entire Bible:

> To Me, O Israelites, you are just like the Ethiopians—declares the Lord. True, I brought Israel up from the land of Egypt, but also the Philistines from Caphtor and the Arameans from Kir. Behold, the Lord God has His eye upon the sinful kingdom: I will wipe it off the face of the earth! But, I will not wholly wipe out the House of Jacob—declares the Lord. For I will give the order and shake the House of Israel—through all the nations—as one shakes [sand] in a sieve, and not a pebble falls to the ground. All the sinners of My people shall perish by the sword, who boast, "Never shall the evil overtake us or come near us." In that day, I will set up again the fallen booth of David: I will mend its breaches and set up its ruins anew. I will build it firm as in the days of old (9:7-11).

There is nothing special about the exodus from Egypt when Israel is immoral (Rashi, Rabbi Joseph Kara). Amos' prophecy in 1:2-9:7, then, is characterized by God's universalistic concern for morality.

The Book of Amos then concludes with a dramatic about-face, in which God's eternal love of Israel shines forth. God promises Israel's eternality and eventual redemption (Rabbi Eliezer of Beaugency, Rabbi Joseph ibn Caspi). The future "day of God" will eliminate the wicked of Israel, but a righteous remnant will endure and be redeemed. In the end, unlike Sodom, Israel will not be completely eliminated, but instead will be refined into a purely righteous nation and return to its ideal relationship with God.

CONCLUSION

The people of Amos' time wrongly distinguished between people who are "religious" and people who are "moral." They concluded that as long as they went through the proper religious ritual motions, God approved of their actions. They supported their claim by considering their newfound wealth and political power to be divine blessings. They also relied on their faulty understanding of what it means to be God's Chosen People.

Amos forcefully attacked their misconceptions. Morality lies at the very heart of the Torah. God holds all nations accountable for ethical conduct, including Israel. Israel's being God's Chosen People places additional responsibility onto Israel to serve as the model moral nation for the world. God rejects religious rituals unaccompanied by a righteous, moral lifestyle.

Unfortunately, most Israelites failed to heed Amos' warnings, and instead attempted to stifle him (2:11-12; 7:10-17). They were consequently exiled by the Assyrians in the following generation. For the most part, these Ten Lost Tribes continue to be missing. However, Amos' message is as relevant now as then. His prophecies remind the Jewish people of their religious responsibilities to God, to themselves, and to humanity. Many people today, as then, create a dangerous dichotomy between people who are "religious" and people who are "moral." Amos returns to the Torah's message, that being God-fearing necessarily means rising to the highest levels of morality and social responsibility. When Israel and the nations understand and embody this teaching, redemption is here.

NOTES

1. In this essay, I draw from the classical Jewish commentators, including Rashi (Rabbi Solomon ben Isaac, 1040-1105), Rabbi Joseph Kara (1050-1125), Rabbi Abraham ibn Ezra (1089-1164), Radak (Rabbi David Kimhi, 1160-c. 1235), Rabbi Eliezer of Beaugency (12ᵗʰ century), Rabbi Joseph ibn Caspi (1279-1340), Rabbi Isaac Abarbanel (1437-1508), and Malbim (Rabbi Meir Leibush ben Yehiel Michel, 1809-1879). I also integrate contemporary scholarship, most notably Amos Hakham, *Da'at Mikra: Amos* in *Twelve Prophets* vol. 1 (Hebrew) (Jerusalem: Mossad HaRav Kook, 1990); Francis I. Andersen & David Noel Freedman, *Amos* Anchor Bible (New York: Doubleday, 1989); Shalom M. Paul, *Mikra LeYisrael: Amos* (Hebrew) (Tel Aviv, Am Oved, 1994); Zev Weissman, et al., *Olam HaTanakh: Twelve Prophets* (Hebrew), (Tel Aviv, Dodson-Iti, 1997).

2. See further discussion in Hayyim Angel, "Was Sodom Destroyed by an Earthquake? A Study of Biblical Earthquakes and Their Implications in Biblical Theology," in Angel, *Through an Opaque Lens*, revised second edition (New York: Kodesh Press, 2013), pp. 123-134.

3. The wicked city of Sodom becomes the biblical epitome of evil (see, for example, Deuteronomy 32:32; Isaiah 3:9; Jeremiah 23:14; Lamentations 4:6). It also serves as the symbol of God's total destruction of evildoers (see, for example, Deuteronomy 29:17-22; Isaiah 1:9; 13:9; Jeremiah 50:40; Amos 4:11).

4. Amos does not explicitly mention Israel as the victim when describing the immoral sins of the Philistines and Tyre (1:6-10). Nevertheless, most commentators reasonably assume that Amos is describing their conduct toward Israel.

5. *Da'at Mikra: Amos*, p. 16.

6. *Da'at Mikra: Amos*, pp. 13, 28-29, 36-37. See also Amos 4:4; 5:5; 8:14. Rashi, Rabbi Joseph Kara, Ibn Ezra, Radak, and several other classical commentators interpret these references as related to idol-worship, but it is unclear that Amos ever explicitly condemns idol-worship.

7. See also, for example, I Samuel 15:22-23; Isaiah 1:10-17; Jeremiah 7:22; Hosea 6:6; Micah 6:4-8; Psalms 51:18-21.

8. Shemuel Ahituv discusses the linguistic and conceptual similarities between humble ('-n-v) and poor ('-n-y), which both derive from the same root ('-n-y/'-n-h). Cf. Isaiah 29:19; Psalms 22:25-27; 69:33-34, where the two terms appear together as poetic parallels (*Mikra LeYisrael: Zephaniah* [Hebrew] [Tel Aviv: Am Oved, 2006], pp. 31-32).

9. See Hayyim Angel, "'The Chosen People': An Ethical Challenge," *Conversations* 27 (Winter 2017), pp. 38-47.

10. *Da'at Mikra: Amos*, p. 44.

GOD INSISTS ON TRUTH:

RABBINIC EVALUATIONS OF TWO AUDACIOUS BIBLICAL PRAYERS*

This article will consider the diversity of response to two sharply formulated prayers in Tanakh. Habakkuk appears to accuse God of poor judgment by allowing the wicked Babylonians to conquer Judah. He then boldly demands a response. Psalm 89 lashes out at God for abrogating the permanent covenant He had struck with the Davidic dynasty.

Traditional interpreters assume that everything in Tanakh is divinely inspired and is applicable to all later generations (see *Megillah* 14a). At the same time, several midrashim and later exegetes are uncomfortable with the bluntness of these prayers and therefore attempt to restrict their applicability. These commentators adopt variations of at least five options:

1. The prophet/psalmist acted religiously appropriately, and therefore we should emulate his prayer.

2. The prophet/psalmist acted religiously appropriately, but most people have not attained a sufficiently high spiritual level to emulate that kind of prayer. Therefore they should speak more diffidently before God.

3. The prophet/psalmist himself was objectively wrong.

4. The prophet/psalmist was quoting someone else rather than speaking for himself.

* This essay appeared originally in the *Jewish Bible Quarterly* 38:1 (2010), pp. 3–9.

5. The text needs to be supplemented or reinterpreted in order to remove the sting of the more literal reading.

HABAKKUK

How long, O Lord, shall I cry out and You not listen, shall I shout to You, "Violence!" And You not save? Why do You make me see iniquity [why] do You look upon wrong? — Raiding and violence are before me, strife continues and contention goes on. That is why decision fails and justice never emerges; for the villain hedges in the just man—therefore judgment emerges deformed (Habakkuk 1:2–4).

I will stand on my watch, take up my station at the post, and wait to see what He will say to me, what He will reply to my complaint (Habakkuk 2:1).[1]

Habakkuk had difficulty with the favor God was to show the Babylonians at the time of the destruction of the Temple. Although Israel may have deserved punishment for its sins, this punishment should not have come at the hands of a nation far more wicked (Abarbanel on 1:13). Habakkuk believed that the success of the wicked Babylonians would reduce faithfulness, since people would conclude that there is no justice in the world (Ibn Ezra, Radak on 1:4). Additionally, Habakkuk expresses frustration that God had not yet responded to his prayers, suggesting a long history of protest prior to the opening of the biblical book.

One midrash is uncomfortable with Habakkuk's tone and sharply criticizes him:

"Keep your mouth from being rash" (Ecclesiastes 5:1) — When Habakkuk said, "I will stand on my watch, Take up my station at the post" (Habakkuk 2:1).... This teaches that he drew a form, and stood in its midst. He said "I will not move from here until You answer me."... God replied, "You are not an ignoramus, but a Torah scholar!"... When Habakkuk heard this, he fell on his face and supplicated. He said, "Master of the Universe! Do not judge me as a willful transgressor, but as an inadvertent sinner [shogeg]." This is what is written, "A prayer of the prophet Habakkuk. In the mode of *Shigionot*" (Habakkuk 3:1) (*Midrash Psalms* 7:17).

This midrash deems Habakkuk guilty of speaking rashly before God, emulating an ignoramus rather than a prophet. It proceeds to explain Habakkuk 3—prefaced with *al shigionot* (midrashically explained as deriving from *sh-g-g*, "error")—as a psalm of repentance by the prophet.[2]

A different approach is espoused in the Talmud (*Ta'anit* 23a), where Habakkuk's story is likened to that of Honi the Circle Drawer: "[Honi] thereupon drew a circle and stood within it in the same way as the prophet Habakkuk had done." Both brazenly and successfully demanded responses from God. Habakkuk received his theological answer, and Honi got the rain he had demanded. Despite Honi's success, however, Shimon ben Shetah was deeply concerned with his conduct:

> If you were not Honi I would have excommunicated you.... But what can I do to you who acts petulantly before the Omnipresent and He grants your desire, as a son who acts petulantly before his father and he grants his desires (*Ta'anit* 23a).

Shimon ben Shetah believed that it is religiously inappropriate to make such demands of God. Nevertheless, he recognized that

Honi enjoyed a unique relationship with God.[3] This talmudic passage appears to espouse the view that Habakkuk and Honi were objectively correct in their prayers. Shimon ben Shetah, concerned that others might emulate them, restricted the applicability of these prayers to an exclusive elite.[4]

Ibn Ezra (on Habakkuk 1:1, 12) adopts a different approach to Habakkuk's prayers. Rather than admit that a prophet spoke those words himself, Ibn Ezra asserts that Habakkuk was quoting others of his generation. Thus Ibn Ezra avoids the need to ask whether this prophetic prayer may be used as a model or not, since Habakkuk was not the originator of those words. Habakkuk still expresses the religious concern of the righteous of his generation and requests a divine answer to their problem, but the prophet himself is not bothered by the theological difficulty of the impending Babylonian victory.

Then again, perhaps Habakkuk spoke for himself, concerned about the religious ramifications the destruction likely would cause. Most commentators do not ascribe these words to other speakers, nor do they think Habakkuk repented in chapter 3. Additionally, God responded directly to Habakkuk without any tone of criticism. Therefore Habakkuk's prayer may have been fully appropriate and may serve as a model for anyone, and God's positive response supports this view.[5]

PSALM 89

Yet You have rejected, spurned, and become enraged at Your anointed. You have repudiated the covenant with Your servant; You have dragged his dignity in the dust. You have breached all his defenses, shattered his strongholds (Psalm 89:39–41).

Psalm 89 is one of the most jarring of the psalms. For 38 verses, the psalmist speaks elatedly of God's eternal covenant with the Davidic monarchy. God swore that it would endure forever, like the sun, moon, and heavens. But then the psalm turns abruptly in verses 39–52, as the psalmist explodes at the abrogation of the covenant when the monarchy ended. It appears that the psalmist is directly accusing God of violating His oath.

Rashi and Meiri attempt to mitigate the protest by inserting an admission of sin: "You have been meticulous with [David's] descendants to weigh their sins until You rejected and spurned them in the time of Zedekiah." In this reading, the psalmist is shifting blame onto Israel, rather than accusing God. However, the flow of the psalm appears to militate against this reading. While the psalmist admits that sin would elicit punishment, the monarchy itself was supposed to endure:

> I will establish his line forever, his throne, as long as the heavens last. If his sons forsake My Teaching and do not live by My rules; if they violate My laws, and do not observe My commands, I will punish their transgression with the rod, their iniquity with plagues. But I will not take away My steadfast love from him; I will not betray My faithfulness (Psalm 89:30–34).[6]

Nevertheless, one can appreciate why these commentators reinterpreted the verses. The plain sense of the text is sharp indeed.

Those who accept the simplest reading must confront this challenge directly. Ibn Ezra (on 89:2) refers to a Spanish sage who considered this psalm blasphemous and therefore censored it: "In Spain, there was a great and pious sage, and this psalm was difficult for him. He would not read it, nor was he able to listen to it since the psalmist speaks sharply against God...." Ibn Ezra agrees that those verses are blasphemous, but he is unwilling to entertain the possibility that an inspired biblical psalmist would speak inappropriately. Therefore he asserts that the psalmist is quoting the words of the enemies of God who blaspheme.

Radak, in turn, censures the anonymous sage and Ibn Ezra:

> Many have expressed astonishment over how this psalmist could speak these words against God [he then quotes the anonymous sage and Ibn Ezra—HA].... I am astonished by their astonishment, for the psalms were written through divine inspiration, and it is unthinkable that something in them is untrue! (Radak on 89:39).

Rabbi Isaiah of Trani and Amos Hakham likewise consider these to be the authentic words of the psalmist. By definition, the words are religiously acceptable, since they appear in the mouth of a divinely inspired writer. Providing a framework for these harsh words, Hakham quotes talmudic passages stating that the righteous do not flatter God. Rather, they stand honestly before their Creator, pouring out all their emotions.[7] Does this mean that everyone may emulate this style of prayer? That is a matter of debate, as we discussed in the case of Habakkuk. In practice, Jewish liturgy did not include this psalm.

GOD INSISTS ON TRUTH

Ever sensitive to minor nuances, the Talmud compares the formulations of four verses scattered throughout Tanakh:

> For the Lord your God is God supreme and Lord supreme, the *great*, the *mighty*, and the *awesome* God (Deuteronomy 10:17).

> O *great* and *mighty* God whose name is Lord of Hosts (Jeremiah 32:18).

121

O Lord, *great* and *awesome* God, who stays faithful to His covenant with those who love Him and keep His commandments! (Daniel 9:4).

And now, our God, *great, mighty,* and *awesome* God, who stays faithful to His covenant (Nehemiah 9:32).

Focusing on the fact that Moses had said "the great, the mighty, and the awesome God," the Sages recognized that Jeremiah and Daniel used only parts of that formulation and that the leaders of the prayer in Nehemiah 9 returned to Moses' complete formula. They posited the following reasoning behind this development:

Why were they called Men of the Great Assembly? Because they restored the crown of Divine attributes to its ancient completeness. Moses had said, "the great, the mighty, and the awesome God." Then Jeremiah came and said, "Foreigners are destroying His Temple! Where are His awesome deeds?" Therefore he omitted "awesome." Daniel came and said, "Foreigners are enslaving His sons. Where are His mighty deeds?" Therefore he omitted "mighty." But they came and said, On the contrary! He performs mighty deeds by suppressing His wrath.... He performs awesome deeds, since were it not for the fear of Him, how could one nation persist among the nations! But how could [Jeremiah and Daniel] abolish something established by Moses? R. Eleazar said: Since they know that the Holy One, blessed be He, insists on truth, they would not ascribe false [things] to Him (*Yoma* 69b).

This talmudic passage sensitively balances the tension of truthfulness and deferential respect before God. On the one hand, the Men of the Great Assembly are praised for their optimism and for restoring Moses' account of God's attributes to its original full form.

Indeed, the Talmud gives them the final word, and the first benediction of the Amidah contains this complete formulation. At the same time, however, the Talmud applauds the profound religious integrity of Jeremiah and Daniel.

Throughout biblical tradition, the lions of faith have challenged God—already beginning with Abraham and Moses:

> Far be it from You to do such a thing, to bring death upon the innocent as well as the guilty, so that innocent and guilty fare alike. Far be it from You! Shall not the Judge of all the earth deal justly? (Genesis 18:25).

> Now, if You will forgive their sin [well and good]; but if not, erase me from the record which You have written! (Exodus 32:32).

One talmudic passage captures the daring spirit of Moses' prayer:

> Rabbi Abbahu said: Were it not explicitly written, it would be impossible to say such a thing: this teaches that Moses took hold of the Holy One, blessed be He, like a man who seizes his fellow by his garment and said before Him: Sovereign of the Universe, I will not let You go until You forgive and pardon them (*Berakhot* 32a).

Whether to pray for the manifestation of God's justice, or to intervene on Israel's behalf, prophets and other biblical writers often spoke brazenly before God. Precisely our spiritual heroes—who generally must be emulated—are those who enjoyed the most intimate relationships with God, affording them a certain comfort level that may be too great for most people. The diversity of rabbinic responses to these and related prayers attests to the power of this paradox that likely never will be resolved.

NOTES

1. The Hebrew reads *u-mah ashiv*, "what *I* will respond" to my complaint. Several commentators explain that other people wanted answers to the same questions the prophet had posed to God. Habakkuk therefore demands answers for himself and for the people who were rebuking him (Rashi, Kara, Ibn Ezra, Radak). Alternatively, Menahem Boleh (*Da'at Mikra: Habakkuk*, in *Twelve Prophets*, vol. 2 [Hebrew] [Jerusalem: Mosad ha-Rav Kook, 1990], p. 10), and the NJPS translation above suggest that the verse should be understood as though it read *u-mah yashiv*, "what He [God] would respond" to my complaint. It was modified either by Habakkuk or a later scribe as a euphemism like other *tikkunei soferim*. See also Shemuel Ahituv, *Mikra LeYisrael: Habakkuk* (Tel Aviv: Am Oved, 2006), p. 39; Francis I. Andersen, *Habakkuk Anchor Bible* (New York: Doubleday, 2001), p. 194. On *tikkunei soferim*, see, for example, Saul Lieberman, *Hellenism in Jewish Palestine* (New York: Jewish Theological Seminary, 1950), pp. 28–37; Moshe A. Zipor, "Some Notes on the Origin of the Tradition of the Eighteen *Tiqqune Soperim*," *VT* 44 (1994), pp. 77–102.

2. Rashi and Rabbi Joseph Kara (on 3:1) adopt this midrashic reading. Abarbanel (on 2:4) also criticizes Habakkuk for speaking too sharply. For a survey of views critical of Habakkuk's prayer, see Aron Pinker, "Was Habakkuk Presumptuous?" *Jewish Bible Quarterly* 32 (2004), pp. 27–34. As we will see below, there are indeed those who criticize Habakkuk for his prayer, but there are other means of responding as well.

3. Two pages later in the Talmud, there is further criticism of speaking brazenly before God: "Levi ordained a fast but no rain fell. He thereupon exclaimed: Master of the Universe, You went up and took Your seat on high and have no mercy upon Your children. Rain fell but he became lame. Rabbi Eleazar said: Let a man never address himself in a reproachful manner towards God, seeing that one great man did so and he became lame, namely, Levi" (*Ta'anit* 25a).

4. Cf. Moshe Greenberg's assessment: "These heroes of faith have achieved a standing with God that ordinary mortals do not enjoy.... The

situation of the ordinary mortal is quite different. With neither a vocation to God's service nor the heroism of these figures of legend, self-assertiveness and autonomy in relation to God would be considered presumptuous... the storming of heaven by prophets hardly served as a model for the ordinary (or even the extraordinary) pious Israelite" ("On the Refinement of the Conception of Prayer in Hebrew Scriptures," *Association for Jewish Studies Review* 1 [1976], p. 58).

5. Francis I. Andersen (*Habakkuk* Anchor Bible, p. 133) observes that there are no instances in Tanakh where God rebukes someone for questioning God's justice. In the Book of Job, God criticizes Job's shortsightedness but vindicates his justness as well. It is worth noting that one psalmist does rebuke those who question God's ways (Psalm 94:8–10), and that type of rebuke is unique in Psalms.

6. This passage alludes to Nathan's prophecy to David in II Samuel 7:12-16. For further discussion of God's covenant with the Davidic dynasty and the effects of sin on the endurance of the kingship, see Hayyim Angel, "The Eternal Davidic Covenant in II Samuel Chapter 7 and Its Later Manifestations in the Bible," in Angel, *The Keys to the Palace: Essays Exploring the Religious Value of Reading the Bible* (New York: Kodesh Press, 2017), pp. 211-223.

7. Amos Hakham, *Da'at Mikra: Psalms* vol. 2 (Hebrew), (Jerusalem: Mosad ha-Rav Kook, 1979) pp. 156–157. See, for example, JT *Berakhot* 7:4 (11c); BT *Yoma* 69b.

TANAKH AND SEPHARDIC INCLUSION IN THE YESHIVA HIGH SCHOOL CURRICULUM*

EDUCATIONAL VISION

God's revealed word in Tanakh lies at the very heart of Jewish thought and religious experience. Educators of Tanakh have the singular opportunity to give their students tools and knowledge to grow throughout their lifetime. The principles we apply in Tanakh education can and should have a meaningful impact on all religious education.

Commentators of Tanakh lived in different lands and throughout the ages. Most of what we learn in the realm of Tanakh has nothing to do with Sephardic, Ashkenazic, or other Jewish communities.[1] We study our commentators because each one enriches our understanding of Tanakh and can deepen our religious experience and engagement.

This point should serve as a guiding principle for all religious education. Students should consider all great rabbinic thinkers and Tanakh commentators as relevant. They also should understand that the more voices we have access to, the broader and deeper our religious experience. This educational worldview also serves to

---

* This essay appeared originally in *Insights from the Sephardic Tradition: An Educational Guide*, ed. Marc D. Angel (New York: Institute for Jewish Ideas and Ideals, 2019), pp. 1-49.

126

unify the Jewish people by teaching that there are many legitimate avenues into tradition.

Reflecting on this aspect of this educational vision, Rabbi Marc D. Angel argues:

> We study this diverse and rich literature and realize the phenomenon that all these Jewish sages and their communities operated with the identical assumption—that God gave the Torah to the people of Israel, that halakha is our way of following God's ways. As we contemplate the vast scope of the halakhic enterprise—and its essential unity—we begin to sense the wholeness of the Jewish people.[2]

There are three areas in Jewish education where we can develop this premise:

- Tanakh must play a prominent role in the general curricular philosophy.

- Even as we may focus heavily on classical medieval commentary and more contemporary approaches, we should intentionally expose high school students to a greater diversity of interpreters and mention where and when they lived.

- We should make brief mention of various customs within learning Tanakh when relevant. This approach teaches respect for diversity, since different communities developed different means of expressing religious experience within *halakhah*.

In the realm of general curricular philosophy, Rabbi Daniel Bouskila explores the approach of Rabbi Benzion Meir Hai Uziel (1880-1953).[3] Born in Jerusalem, Rabbi Uziel served as Chief Rabbi of Tel-Aviv from 1911 to 1921, and then was Chief Rabbi of Salonika (Thessaloniki) for two years. In 1923, he returned to Israel and assumed the post of Chief Rabbi of Tel-Aviv. From 1939 until his death in 1953, he was the Sephardic Chief Rabbi, the Rishon LeZion, of Israel. He served as Chief Rabbi during the founding of the State of Israel and wrote extensively on the halakhic ramifications of the State and the staggering changes in Jewish life it would bring.

Rabbi Uziel believed that what he considered to be a Sephardic-style curriculum should become the intellectual and spiritual framework for the entire Jewish people. His vision was based on a religious-intellectual approach, rather than the ethnic background of students. His goal was to unite Jews through Torah, rather than promoting ethnic separations. Rabbi Bouskila quotes one of Rabbi Uziel's remarks from his 50th birthday gathering in 1930:

> I love the concept of unity for our people, and my goal is to see the elimination of the unnatural divisions amongst us that were created by the diaspora. I absolutely hate divisiveness, and I sharply condemn and reject all divisiveness masked as religion.

Rabbi Uziel characterized the classical Sephardic curriculum as more focused on talmudic studies aimed at deriving the practical *halakhah*; and an emphasis on Tanakh, Jewish thought, and mysticism, as well as worldly knowledge.

Rabbi Uziel's envisioned curriculum of a classical Sephardic approach that would benefit all Jews is an idealization, and was hardly representative of the entire Sephardic world. In fact, Rabbi Uziel was the head of the venerable Sephardic institution, Yeshivat Porat Yosef in Jerusalem. While most of the Sephardic rabbis in Porat Yosef taught Torah, Talmud, and *halakhah*, Rabbi Uziel distinguished himself by emphasizing Jewish thought and philosophy, and by being an ardent Zionist. What Rabbi Uziel considered the "Sephardic" approach, then, was iconoclastic within his own Sephardic Yeshivah![4] Ideally, Jewish education should be modeled after Rabbi Uziel's "Sephardic" system, characterized by a more holistic approach.[5]

TANAKH

In Tanakh, students should engage with God's word through the guidance of our greatest interpreters and thinkers. We never would learn Tanakh only through the eyes of the Northern French commentators such as Rashi or Rashbam, nor would we draw exclusively from the Spanish interpreters such as Ibn Ezra or Ramban. Nor should we stop with the medieval period of interpretation, given the wealth of insight and scholarship that emerged over the past 500 years. Even if we devote the lion's share of our attention to the classical medieval commentators, there is great value in the periodic mention of later commentators. It is critical to send the message that great thinkers of every age and era have added their voices to the Torah.

There also is a particular gap in contemporary Jewish education regarding Sephardim. Whereas medieval Sephardic interpreters and thinkers are meaningfully studied, post-Expulsion thinkers and interpreters are often ignored. An easy challenge for educators to illustrate this point: Name *five* Sephardic rabbis who lived from 1550-1900. If many religious educators struggle to answer so basic a question, there is little hope that their students will fare any better. This unfortunate educational gap often is manifest throughout the realms of biblical interpretation, *halakhah*, history, and customs.[6]

Later commentators from the Ashkenazic world have fared much better in contemporary Jewish education. Names like Rabbi Eliyahu of Vilna (Gra, 1720-1797), Rabbi Yaakov Tzvi Mecklenburg

(1785-1865), Rabbi Samson Raphael Hirsch (1808-1888), Malbim (Rabbi Meir Leibush ben Yehiel Michel, 1809-1879), Netziv (Rabbi Naftali Zvi Yehudah Berlin, 1817-1893), Rabbi David Zvi Hoffmann (1843-1921), and others rightly have become familiar names to advanced students of Tanakh. In a different arena, the many Hasidic masters and their insightful homiletical approaches such as Rabbi Elimelech of Lizhensk (1717-1786, *Noam Elimelech*), Rabbi Levi Yitzhak of Berditchev (1740-1810, *Kedushat Levi*), Rabbi Yitzhak Meir Alter of Ger (1799-1866, *Hiddushei ha-Rim*), Rabbi Yehudah Aryeh Leib Alter (1847-1905, *Sefat Emet*), and Rabbi Shmuel Bornsztain (1855-1926, *Shem mi-Shemuel*), among many others, have found a meaningful place in religious education and conversation.

It is worth making the extra effort to sprinkle in interpreters from the pan-Sephardic world (which includes Middle Eastern and North African communities that never went through Spain and therefore are not technically "Sephardic").[7] Aside from the valuable contributions these interpreters have made, this educational approach enables students to absorb the message that the pan-Sephardic world meaningfully contributes to our understanding of Tanakh and Jewish experience after the Expulsion from Spain.[8] There is no need to overhaul any curriculum or lesson plan. It simply is about educators being informed, and then adding several comments throughout the year to enrich the discussion and to broaden the playing field of interpretation for their students.

Here are a few examples from pan-Sephardic Tanakh interpreters from the sixteenth to nineteenth centuries that I have found useful in my undergraduate Tanakh courses at Yeshiva University and in my Adult Education classes. These commentators generally do not play a central role in my courses, but their voices should be heard periodically. Needless to say, educators have access to a wealth of interpretation and may cite what they deem most relevant for their own classes.

RABBI AVRAHAM GAVISON (1520-1578, ALGERIA)

Rabbi Avraham Gavison wrote a commentary on the Book of Proverbs entitled *Omer ha-Shik'khah*. He proposed a fascinating theory pertaining to the authorship of the final two chapters of the Book of Proverbs.[9] Although most of the book is explicitly ascribed to King Solomon (Proverbs 1:1; 10:1; 25:1), chapters 30-31 refer to people named Agur, Ithiel, Ucal, and Lemuel:

> The words of Agur son of Jakeh, [man of] Massa; The speech of the man to Ithiel, to Ithiel and Ucal (Proverbs 30:1).

> The words of Lemuel, king of Massa, with which his mother admonished him (Proverbs 31:1).

> Several Midrashim and later commentators assume that Agur and Lemuel are nicknames of Solomon (*Tanhuma* Buber *Vaera* 2, Rashi, Ralbag). Others maintain that these are the names of different wise men (Saadiah Gaon, Rabbi Eliyahu of Vilna).

Rabbi Avraham Gavison proposed that Agur, Ithiel, Ucal, and Lemuel were non-Israelite wise men who came to Israel to learn from Solomon, and then taught the proverbs they had learned from their master. Rabbi Gavison drew on an earlier verse in Proverbs that notes that Hezekiah[10] and his men played an editing role in the book:

> These too are proverbs of Solomon, which the men of King Hezekiah of Judah copied (Proverbs 25:1).

According to Rabbi Gavison, the men of Hezekiah translated the proverbs of Agur, Ithiel, Ucal, and Lemuel back into Hebrew for inclusion in the biblical book, and included them in chapters 30-31. Thus, Solomon still can claim ultimate "authorship" of these proverbs, which were also credited to the non-Israelite sages who learned from Solomon and taught them to others.

RABBI AVRAHAM BEN SHELOMO (16TH CENTURY YEMEN)

David said to Nathan, "I stand guilty before the Lord!" And Nathan replied to David, "The Lord has remitted your sin; you shall not die. However, since you have spurned the enemies of the Lord by this deed, even the child about to be born to you shall die." Nathan went home, and the Lord afflicted the child that Uriah's wife had borne to David, and it became critically ill. David entreated God for the boy; David fasted, and he went in and spent the night lying on the ground. The elder servants of his household tried to induce him to get up from the ground; but he refused, nor would he partake of food with them. On the seventh day the child died. David's servants were afraid to tell David that the child was dead; for they said, "We spoke to him when the child was alive and he wouldn't listen to us; how can we tell him that the child is dead? He might do something terrible." When David saw his servants talking in whispers, David understood that the child was dead; David asked his servants, "Is the child dead?" "Yes," they replied. Thereupon David rose from the ground; he bathed and anointed himself, and he changed his clothes. He went into the House of the Lord and prostrated himself. Then he went home and asked for food, which they set before him, and he ate. His courtiers asked him, "Why have you acted in this manner? While the child was alive, you fasted and wept; but now that the child is dead, you rise and take food!" He replied, "While the child was still alive, I fasted and wept because I thought: 'Who knows? The Lord may have pity on me, and the child may live.' But now that he is dead, why should I fast? Can I bring him back again? I shall go to him, but he will never come back to me" (II Samuel 12:13-23).

Following David's sin with Bathsheba and Uriah, the prophet Nathan condemns him bitterly and pronounces divine punishment. David confesses that he has sinned, embarking on a process of repentance. While this repentance was sufficient to save David's life, Nathan tells David that his infant son from the affair will die. The ensuing narrative goes at length to describe the difference in perspective between David and his courtiers. The latter were shocked at David's change of mood from being emotionally distraught while the infant was ill, but then suddenly becoming calm once the infant died.

Although a number of commentators understand David's strikingly philosophical response at his word, several commentators and contemporary scholars offer different explanations. Abarbanel submits that David knew that the infant would die, but did not want anyone to suspect his affair with Bathsheba; therefore, he acted tormented over his son's illness. Professor Jonathan Jacobs maintains that David understood that his son's illness was a divine punishment, but as long as the child was still alive, David genuinely maintained hope that God would overturn the decree. Of course, David would not share this critical layer of knowledge with his courtiers, and consequently presented a philosophical explanation to them after the infant's death.[11]

A sixteenth-century Yemenite rabbi, Rabbi Avraham ben Shelomo, submits that David wanted the infant, the product of an illicit affair, to die. Once the infant died, David was relieved. When "David entreated God for the boy" (verse 16), he actually prayed for the infant's death. However, David did not want his courtiers to know his true thoughts so he explained to them that he prayed "because I thought: 'Who knows? The Lord may have pity on me, and the child may live'" (verse 22).[12] This interpretation raises a different possible dimension to how David felt toward the offspring of his affair with Bathsheba.

RABBI SHEMUEL LANIADO (DIED 1605, SYRIA)
RABBI MOSHE ALSHEIKH (1508-1593, TURKEY, ISRAEL)

Rabbi Shemuel Laniado's commentary on the Former Prophets, entitled *Keli Yakar*, contains several valuable insights into the Elijah narratives in the Book of Kings.

> Elijah the Tishbite, an inhabitant of Gilead, said to Ahab, "As the Lord lives, the God of Israel whom I serve, there will be no dew or rain except at my bidding." The word of the Lord came to him: "Leave this place; turn eastward and go into hiding by the Wadi Cherith, which is east of the Jordan. You will drink from the wadi, and I have commanded the ravens to feed you there." He proceeded to do as the Lord had bidden: he went, and he stayed by the Wadi Cherith, which is east of the Jordan. The ravens brought him bread and meat every morning and every evening, and he drank from the wadi.
>
> After some time the wadi dried up, because there was no rain in the land. And the word of the Lord came to him: "Go at once to Zarephath of Sidon, and stay there; I have designated a widow there to feed you." So he went at once to Zarephath. When he came to the entrance of the town, a widow was there gathering wood. He called out to her, "Please bring me a little water in your pitcher, and let me drink." As she went to fetch

it, he called out to her, "Please bring along a piece of bread for me." "As the Lord your God lives," she replied, "I have nothing baked, nothing but a handful of flour in a jar and a little oil in a jug. I am just gathering a couple of sticks, so that I can go home and prepare it for me and my son; we shall eat it and then we shall die" (I Kings 17:1-12).

Following Elijah's decree of the drought, God miraculously provided for the prophet and protected him by keeping him in hiding. Rabbi Laniado, however, proposes that God supported Elijah's decree of the drought, but also subtly wished to teach the prophet that the decree was overly harsh. Wadi Cherith is not mentioned elsewhere in Tanakh. Perhaps this name suggests that Elijah needed to be "cut off," *karet*, from society.

When this first lesson was lost on the prophet, God then provided for Elijah by having ravens bring him food. Rabbi Laniado maintains that this species of bird carries symbolic meaning. Ravens are "cruel" in the sense that they do not even provide for their own young. God therefore made them go against their own nature to feed Elijah. So too, God attempted to teach Elijah that he should act against his own nature and rescind the drought.

Rabbi Moshe Alsheikh comments on God's attempting to teach Elijah to be less harsh against Israel despite the rampant idolatry that led the prophet to proclaim the drought. Following the drying up of Wadi Cherith after a year of the drought, God instructs Elijah to head north to Zarephath to the home of a widow and her son who were at the brink of starvation. Rabbi Alsheikh explains that God now wanted Elijah to witness the suffering inflicted on the people from the drought that the prophet had decreed. Even that lesson was lost on the prophet, so God needed to continue to educate the prophet in the ensuing narrative.[13]

RABBI YAAKOV FIDANQUE (17TH CENTURY, AMSTERDAM, LONDON, COMMENTARY ON THE FORMER PROPHETS)

Rabbi Yaakov Fidanque published his commentary within what became the standard edition of Rabbi Yitzhak Abarbanel's commentary on the Former Prophets. His commentary is under the name "Rif." He contributes to the discussion of the overall religious influence of the *shofetim*, or judges-saviors, in the Book of Judges.

In the two appendix stories at the end of the book (chapters 17-21), the Idol of Micah and the Concubine at Gibeah, the narrative establishes a chorus to ascribe the people's sinful behavior to the absence of a king:

> In those days there was no king in Israel; every man did as he pleased (Judges 17:6; 18:1; 19:1; 21:25).

Because the two episodes are undated within the period, commentators debate when they occurred. Many commentators accept the interpretation of the *Seder Olam Rabbah*, that these stories occurred toward the beginning of the period of the judges. Rashi (on Judges 17:1, from *Seder Olam Rabbah* 12) maintains that Micah built his illegal shrine during the tenure of Othniel, the first of the judges (see Judges 3:7-11). Ralbag (on 17:1) disagrees, since the introduction to the Book of Judges suggests that the judges exerted a positive influence over the nation, and the people reverted to their sinful behavior only after the judges died:

> When the Lord raised up chieftains for them, the Lord would be with the chieftain and would save them from their enemies during the chieftain's lifetime; for the Lord would be moved to pity by their moanings because of those who oppressed and

crushed them. But when the chieftain died, they would again act basely, even more than the preceding generation—following other gods, worshiping them, and bowing down to them; they omitted none of their practices and stubborn ways (Judges 2:18-19).

Therefore, Ralbag concludes that the two sinful episodes occurred prior to Othniel, and the lamentation over the absence of a king includes the absence of any judges.

Rabbi Yaakov Fidanque observes that the chorus of verses lamenting the absence of a king refers specifically to kings, and condemns the judges. Accepting the majority rabbinic opinion that the two episodes occurred toward the beginning of that era, Rabbi Fidanque notes that none of the judges eliminated the illegal shrine of Micah, which functioned throughout the period:

They maintained the sculptured image that Micah had made throughout the time that the House of God stood at Shiloh (Judges 18:31).

The Tabernacle remained in Shiloh until the time of Eli at the beginning of the Book of Samuel. Rabbi Fidanque concludes that the influence of even the best of the judges was local, and did not transform the entire nation of Israel.

RABBI HAYYIM IBN ATTAR
(OR HA-HAYYIM, 1696-1743, MOROCCO)

Rabbi Hayyim ibn Attar's commentary on the Torah is included in the standard rabbinic Bibles, the *Mikraot Gedolot*. Although he is heavily influenced by Midrash and Kabbalah, he also advances several *peshat*-driven comments.[14]

In Genesis chapter 14, Abraham heroically battles against four kings and rescues his nephew Lot, who was captured along with his wicked city, Sodom. The Torah relates the aftermath of this battle:

> When he returned from defeating Chedorlaomer and the kings with him, the king of Sodom came out to meet him in the Valley of Shaveh, which is the Valley of the King.

> And King Melchizedek of Salem brought out bread and wine; he was a priest of God Most High. He blessed him, saying, "Blessed be Abram of God Most High, Creator of heaven and earth. And blessed be God Most High, Who has delivered your foes into your hand." And [Abram] gave him a tenth of everything.

> Then the king of Sodom said to Abram, "Give me the persons, and take the possessions for yourself." But Abram said to the king of Sodom, "I swear to the Lord, God Most High, Creator of heaven and earth: I will not take so much as a thread or a sandal strap of what is yours; you shall not say, 'It is I who made Abram rich.' For me, nothing but what my servants have used up; as for the share of the men who went with me—Aner, Eshkol, and Mamre—let them take their share" (Genesis 14:17-24).

The flow of the text is puzzling. When the king of Sodom comes to greet Abraham (verse 17), we expect that he will then speak. Instead, there is an interruption containing an exchange between Melchizedek and Abraham (verses 18-20). Only then does the narrative resume with the dialogue between Abraham and the king of Sodom (verses 21-24).

Rabbi Hayyim ibn Attar explains that the interruption illustrates what the king of Sodom *should* have said and done after Abraham risked his life to save his city. Instead, the righteous Melchizedek expresses gratitude, generosity, and thankfulness to God for the heroic rescue. The insertion of the exchange between Abraham and Melchizedek serves to highlight the disappointingly cold response of the wicked king of Sodom.

In a different example, Rabban Gamliel famously explains the symbol of bitter herbs (*maror*) eaten on Passover as a reminiscence of the bitter experience in Egypt (Mishnah, *Pesahim* 10:5, quoted in the Passover Haggadah). However, Rabbi Hayyim ibn Attar (on Exodus 12:8) explains that at the level of *peshat*, the bitter herb is simply a delicious pungent condiment that enhances the flavor of the Passover sacrifice of lamb or goat with the matzah. The midrashic interpretation of Rabban Gamliel does not reflect the original meaning of the commandment.

RABBI RAPHAEL BERDUGO (1747-1821, MOROCCO)

Rabbi Raphael Berdugo was deeply committed to the pursuit of *peshat* in his commentary on the Former Prophets, entitled *Mesammehei Lev*.[15] He offers a fascinating interpretation of the post-Goliath jealousy of Saul toward David that arose from the poetic praises of the women after the battle:

When the [troops] came home [and] David returned from killing the Philistine, the women of all the towns of Israel came out singing and dancing to greet King Saul with timbrels, shouting, and sistrums. The women sang as they danced, and they chanted: "Saul has slain his thousands; David, his tens of thousands!" Saul was much distressed and greatly vexed about the matter. For he said, "To David they have given tens of thousands, and to me they have given thousands. All that he lacks is the kingship!" From that day on Saul kept a jealous eye on David (I Samuel 18:6-9).

Most commentators assume that Saul understood the women's words correctly and subsequently became jealous. However, Rabbi Berdugo submits that Saul *misinterpreted* the victory song of the women. In biblical poetry, the smaller number generally is placed first in a poetic parallelism (see, for example, Deuteronomy 32:30; Psalm 91:7). The women respectfully placed Saul before David since Saul was king. They associated Saul with thousands, and David with tens of thousands, since the smaller number comes first in biblical poetry. Saul, however, misinterpreted the poem as suggesting that David was the greater hero for killing a larger number of Israel's enemies. Several contemporary scholars also consider this interpretation a viable possibility.[16]

RABBI ELIYAHU BENAMOZEGH (ITALY, 1823-1900)

Rabbi Eliyahu Benamozegh was a remarkable figure whose primary contribution in Jewish thought pertains to his keen interest in the relationship between Judaism and other world religions. He made a strong philosophical case for the universal relevance of Jewish values.[17]

He composed a commentary on the Torah, *Em la-Mikra*. In this work, he incorporated the findings of philology, archaeology, and comparative studies with ancient Greek mythology. He maintained that Jewish tradition could be enriched by studying traditions that were alien to it. His commentary was condemned and banned by more conservative rabbis in Aleppo and Damascus for being too open to external sciences and to Greek mythology. In response, Rabbi Benamozegh composed an impassioned defense of his Orthodoxy. Although his biblical scholarship in this area is obviously dated, his general approach to the interface between tradition and contemporary scholarship is as relevant as ever.

RABBI YAAKOV HULI
(ME'AM LO'EZ, ISRAEL, TURKEY, 1689-1732)

Although not a Tanakh commentator in the manner of the other figures discussed in this section, we must mention the remarkable contribution of Rabbi Yaakov Huli. He composed the *Me'am Lo'ez* anthology in Ladino (Judeo-Spanish)—the language spoken by the Jews of much of the Ottoman Empire at that time. He wanted those who could not understand classical commentaries in Hebrew, to have access to the wealth of traditional commentary and law in their vernacular. Although the compendium is not an original commentary, the idea of a popular work for the masses was groundbreaking. Tragically, Rabbi Huli died at age 43, and therefore completed only the work on Genesis and most of Exodus. Later rabbis, inspired by his vision, completed the entire work. The *Me'am Lo'ez* was an immediate success, and continues to be studied in the original Ladino as well as in Hebrew and English translations today.[18]

SEVERAL OTHER RABBINIC COMMENTARIES

Of course, the list of rabbis who wrote commentaries on parts of Tanakh can extend far beyond those mentioned above.[19]

- Rabbi Eliyahu Mizrahi (1455-1525, Constantinople, *Sefer ha-Mizrahi*, a supercommentary on Rashi's commentary on the Torah)
- Rabbi Moshe Almosnino (1515-1580, Salonika)
- Rabbi Vidal HaTzarfati (1540-1619, Morocco)
- Rabbi Aharon ibn Hayyim (1545-1632, Morocco, Egypt)
- Rabbi Menassheh ben Israel (1604-1657, Amsterdam)

- Rabbi Hayyim Abulafia (1660-1774, Israel, Turkey)

- Rabbi Moshe Berdugo (1679-1730, Morocco)

- Rabbi Yehudah Berdugo (1689-1744, Morocco)

- Rabbi Hayyim Yosef David Azulai (1724-1801, Israel, Italy)

- Rabbi Yitzhak Shemuel Reggio (1784-1855, Gorizia, Italy)

- Rabbi Eliezer Papo (1785-1828, Sarajevo, Bulgaria)

- Rabbi Hayyim Palachi (1788-1868, Turkey)

- Rabbi Yaakov Abuhatzeira (1806-1880, Morocco)

- Rabbi Vidal Coenca (1810-1862, Salonika, Israel)

- Rabbi Yosef Hayyim of Baghdad (*Ben Ish Hai*, 1835-1909)

- Rabbi Yeshuah HaLevi of Gilbraltar (born 1836)

- Rabbi Ezra Reuven Dangoor (1848-1930, Iraq)

- Rabbi Yom Tov Yedid Halevi (1856-1923, Syria)

- Rabbi Yaakov Hai Zerihen (1869-1953, Israel)

- Rabbi David Tzabah (1869-1956, Morocco)

- Rabbi Yismah Ovadiah (1872-1952, Morocco)

- Rabbi Yaish Krispin (1875-1939, Morocco)

- Rabbi Yosef Ben Naim (1882-1951, Morocco)

- Rabbi Mahalel HaAdani (1883-1950, Yemen)

- Rabbi Barukh Avraham Toledano (1890-1970, Morocco)

CONCLUDING REMARKS ON TANAKH COMMENTARY

On a practical level, educators should read contemporary commentaries and anthologies that cite many works from different eras. Nehama Leibowitz's *Studies* are classics in this area. A contemporary valuable online resource is alhatorah.org, by Rabbi Hillel Novetsky.

The essays on each topic survey and analyze a wealth of classical and contemporary approaches, making access to many of the more obscure commentators easy for educators.

The more commentaries educators have in their own arsenal, the more they can fathom Tanakh texts. They also are better equipped to provide more avenues for students to connect to tradition and to respect legitimate diversity within a commitment to Torah. Moreover, by teaching students that interpretation of Tanakh comes from many lands and eras, our students can identify with all Jewish thought, thinkers, and history.

It is not of primary importance for high school students to memorize the name, dates, or place of every rabbi. However, educators can create the proper environment for students to taste from the vast wellsprings of tradition and see that many voices contribute to the discussion.

MENTION OF DIVERSE CUSTOMS
IN THE CONTEXT OF TANAKH LEARNING

There are regular opportunities for Tanakh educators to mention different customs in the context of their classes. These educational moments serve to generate respect for different approaches into tradition. Below are a few examples.

PSALMS

A psalm of David. A song for the dedication of the House. I extol You, O Lord, for You have lifted me up, and not let my enemies rejoice over me. O Lord, my God, I cried out to You, and You healed me. O Lord, You brought me up from Sheol, preserved me from going down into the Pit (Psalm 30:1-4).

Students who learn Psalm 30 confront questions that have baffled commentators for millennia. David did not build the Temple (the initial explanation of "the House" in verse 1), and it also is difficult to ascertain the connection between the title verse and the body of the psalm. It sounds like the psalm expresses gratitude for salvation from some mortal danger. What is the relevance of that theme to the dedication of the Temple?

In a class on Psalms, educators may turn to the commentators who propose a number of approaches to solve these difficulties.[20] At some point during that analysis, it is valuable to mention that while Sephardim and Ashkenazim recite this psalm on a daily basis, Sephardim generally omit the title verse from the prayer (and begin with verse 2, "I extol you"), and therefore do not have to confront these difficult interpretive questions on a daily basis. Educators may furnish a liturgical parallel from the Ashkenazic practice to omit the title verse of Psalm 6, which they recite in the supplicatory prayers (*tahanun*). Instead, they begin with verse 2, "O Lord, do not punish...":

> For the leader; with instrumental music on the *sheminith*. A psalm of David. O Lord, do not punish me in anger, do not chastise me in fury (Psalm 6:1-2).

Finally, educators can note that Sephardim generally recite Psalm 25, rather than Psalm 6, in their supplicatory prayers.

By appending a brief discussion of these customs to a text analysis of Psalm 30, educators are able to highlight several critical issues in daily prayer and connect those two realms for their students.[21]

To cite a different example, the *Pesukei de-Zimra/Zemirot* offer psalms of praise to draw us into the proper religious mindset for the mandatory prayers—the Shema, the Amidah, and their associated blessings. On Shabbat morning, Sephardim read the psalms in order of their appearance in the Book of Psalms. Ashkenazim read the psalms in a different order, presumably arranged for thematic reasons. Rabbi Shalom Carmy wrote an article offering a conceptual explanation for the Ashkenazic arrangement.[22] To understand the reasoning behind the order of the Sephardic liturgy, just open a Tanakh!

In a similar vein, in Minhah of Shabbat, Sephardim and Ashkenazim usually recite three verses beginning with *tzidkatekha* after the Amidah. Once again, Sephardim recite these verses in their order of appearance in Psalms (36:7; 71:19; 119:142). Ashkenazim reverse the order, requiring explanation. Rabbi Yehoshua Falk (1555-1614, *Perishah* on *Tur Orah Hayyim* 292:6) suggests that God's ineffable Name does not appear in 119:142; Elokim appears twice in 71:19; and God's ineffable Name (Y-H-V-H) appears in 36:7. Therefore, Ashkenazim read the verses in an ascending order of holiness. Others suggest that Ashkenazim arranged the verses so that God's Name is the last word preceding the Kaddish.[23]

HAFTAROT

Although the Sages of the Talmud codified the prophetic passages to be read as *haftarot* for holidays, they left the choice of regular Shabbat *haftarot* to the discretion of individual communities (Rabbi Yosef Karo, *Kesef Mishneh* on Rambam, *Hilkhot Tefillah* 12:12). Consequently, several *haftarah* reading traditions have arisen.

Frequently, when Sephardim and Ashkenazim read from same passage, Sephardim read a shorter *haftarah*. In *Parashat Beshallah*, for example, Sephardim read Deborah's song in Judges chapter 5, whereas Ashkenazim read the chapter of the Deborah narrative beforehand as well. Sephardim thereby highlight the Song at the Sea in the *parashah*, whereas Ashkenazim draw on the broader parallel with narrative and song in both.

A striking example of the phenomenon of Sephardim choosing a shorter passage is the *haftarah* of *Parashat Vayera*. II Kings, chapter 4 relates the story of the prophet Elisha and an anonymous woman from Shunem who offered him hospitality. Elisha prophesied that this woman would give birth to a son, and indeed she did. These themes directly parallel elements of the *parashah*: angelic guests visit Abraham and Sarah; Abraham and Sarah offer their guests hospitality; the angels promise them the birth of Isaac; and Isaac is born.

After these initial parallels to the *parashah*, the story in the *haftarah* takes a tragic turn in verses 18–23. The son dies, and the woman goes to find Elisha. As she leaves home, the woman's husband asks why she was going out if it was not a special occasion, and she replies, "*Shalom*." This is where Sephardim end the *haftarah*. Ashkenazim read the continuation of the narrative in verses 24–37, in which the woman finds Elisha who returns to her house and God miraculously revives the child. It is jarring that Sephardim conclude the *haftarah* at a point where the child still is lifeless rather than proceeding to the happy and miraculous ending of the story.

Rabbi Elhanan Samet justifies the abrupt conclusion by noting that the entire story is inordinately long for a congregational setting (37 verses). Sephardim therefore limited the *haftarah* to 23 verses at the expense of reading to its happy ending. They conclude with the word "*Shalom*" to strike at least some positive note. In contrast, Ashkenazim favored completing the story even though that meant reading a very lengthy *haftarah* in synagogue.[24]

The *haftarah* of *Parashat Shemot* is an example where Sephardim, Ashkenazim, and Yemenites adopted passages from different prophetic books to highlight different themes from the *parashah*.

146

Sephardim read the beginning of the Book of Jeremiah (1:1–2:3). In this passage, God selects Jeremiah as a prophet. Jeremiah expresses reluctance only to be rebuffed by God:

> I replied: Ah, Lord God! I don't know how to speak, for I am still a boy. And the Lord said to me: Do not say, I am still a boy, but go wherever I send you and speak whatever I command you (Jeremiah 1:6–7).

This choice of *haftarah* focuses on the parallels between Jeremiah's initiation and ensuing reluctance, and Moses' hesitation in accepting his prophetic mission in the *parashah*.

Ashkenazim read from the Book of Isaiah, focusing primarily on the theme of national redemption:

> [In days] to come Jacob shall strike root, Israel shall sprout and blossom, and the face of the world shall be covered with fruit (Isaiah 27:6).

> For when he—that is, his children—behold what My hands have wrought in his midst, they will hallow My name. Men will hallow the Holy One of Jacob and stand in awe of the God of Israel (Isaiah 29:23).

Although there is rebuke in the middle of the *haftarah*, the passage begins and ends with consolation and redemption.

Yemenites read one of Ezekiel's harsh diatribes against Israel for their infidelity to God. The prophet compares them to an unfaithful woman who has cheated on God by turning to idolatry and the allures of pagan nations:

> "O mortal, proclaim Jerusalem's abominations to her" (Ezekiel 16:2).[25]

Ashkenazim highlight the link between the national exile and redemption. Yemenites read Ezekiel's caustic condemnation of the Israelites, implying that the Israelites *deserved* slavery as a punishment for having assimilated in Egypt. It likely was used as an exhortation to contemporary Jews to remain faithful to the Torah. Sephardim focus on the central figure of the *parashah*—Moses.

When teaching *Parashat Shemot*, educators have a singular opportunity to use the various customs to highlight major themes in the *parashah* and to teach diversity of custom throughout the Jewish community.

STANDING OR SITTING
DURING THE TEN COMMANDMENTS

The Revelation at Sinai is the only time in human history that God spoke directly to an entire nation, and it forms the eternal foundation for the God-Israel relationship. It is fair to say that this passage is the most important passage in the Torah.

At an early stage, the Ten Commandments were a central part of the daily liturgy, recited next to the Shema (Mishnah, *Tamid* 5:1). However, the Talmud (*Berakhot* 12a) reports that a heretical sect claimed that God revealed *only* the Ten Commandments, but not the rest of the Torah. To distance their community from this heretical idea, the Rabbis eliminated the reading of the Ten Commandments from the daily liturgy.

Later Jewish tradition thus inherited two critical principles: (1) The Ten Commandments is the most important passage of the Torah; (2) God revealed the entire Torah, and it is undesirable to do anything that might suggest that God revealed only the Ten Commandments. Communities responded to the balance of these principles in different ways. Many Ashkenazic communities retained the practice of standing during the reading of the Ten Commandments, re-enacting the Revelation and stressing that this passage is of singular importance. Many Sephardic communities, by contrast, adopted the practice to remain seated during the reading of the Ten Commandments, so as not to make it appear that this passage is more important than the rest of the Torah.[26]

THE PRIESTLY BLESSING:
DAILY RECITAL OR ONLY ON HOLIDAYS?

The Lord spoke to Moses: Speak to Aaron and his sons: Thus shall you bless the people of Israel. Say to them: The Lord bless you and protect you! The Lord deal kindly and graciously with you! The Lord bestow His favor upon you and grant you peace! Thus they shall link My name with the people of Israel, and I will bless them (Numbers 6:22-27).

In the context of teaching the Priestly Blessing, educators may observe that this commandment appears to be applicable anywhere, and is not specifically restricted to the Temple. However, there is a widespread custom among Ashkenazic communities to recite the Priestly Blessing in synagogue only on Yom Tov (Rama, *Orah Hayyim* 128:44).

In his *Bet Yosef*, Rabbi Yosef Karo expresses astonishment at the Ashkenazic practice. How could they reduce the fulfillment of a Torah commandment? Rama (Rabbi Moshe Isserles) justifies the custom by explaining that people are stressed about their work during the week, and the stress persists even on Shabbat. On holidays, however, they are in a better mood. Still, how could they modify a daily Torah commandment? Several Ashkenazic halakhists, including Rabbi Eliyahu of Vilna (Gra, 1720-1797, who unsuccessfully attempted to return the custom to a daily recital[27]) and Rabbi Yehiel Michel Epstein (1829-1908, *Arukh ha-Shulhan*) also criticized the prevalent Ashkenazic practice.[28]

Rabbi Elhanan Samet[29] suggests that one must locate the rationale for the Ashkenazic practice in the assumption that the Priestly Blessing today is a rabbinic commandment, not a biblical one. Rabbi Samet suggests that the fundamental difference between reciting the Priestly Blessing in the Temple as opposed to anywhere else is in the use of God's ineffable Name (*Shem ha-Meforash*). Certain verses stress this element:

> At that time the Lord set apart the tribe of Levi to carry the Ark of the Lord's Covenant, to stand in attendance upon the Lord, *and to bless in His name*, as is still the case (Deuteronomy 10:8).

> The priests, sons of Levi, shall come forward; for the Lord your God has chosen them to minister to Him and *to pronounce blessing in the name of the Lord*, and every lawsuit and case of assault is subject to their ruling (Deuteronomy 21:5).

Evidently, certain medieval Ashkenazic authorities interpreted this aspect of the Priestly Blessing as essential to fulfilling the Torah commandment. Ashkenazic communities could reduce the number of recitals because they believed that the Priestly Blessing today is a rabbinic commandment absent the Temple. The widespread Sephardic position, championed by Rambam, the *Shulhan Arukh*, and many others, is that God's ineffable Name could be uttered only in the Temple, but that is not an essential component of the Torah commandment of the Priestly Blessing. Therefore, the Priestly Blessing today is a Torah commandment, and must be recited daily.

OTHER CUSTOMS

In general, educators should note which communities practice a certain custom, rather than saying that "we" or "Jews" do something. Within the realm of the *Megillot*, many Ashkenazic Jews chant the words *ve-kelim mi-kelim shonim*, "beakers of varied design" (Esther 1:7), to the tune of the Book of Lamentations. This custom derives from a midrashic teaching that King Ahasuerus used the utensils from the Temple at his parties (*Megillah* 12a, *Esther Rabbah* 2:1). However, Sephardic communities do not have this custom.

Similarly, many Ashkenazic communities, and a number of Sephardic communities, read the Book of Ecclesiastes on Sukkot. However, many Sephardic communities do not. The more specific formulation of which communities have a certain custom is both more accurate and also does not subtly invalidate the practices of students and entire communities that have their own sacred customs and traditions.[30]

To enhance the learning environment, all educators should own and read through different prayer books, pay attention to the *haftarah* notes regarding which communities read which passages, and have a general appreciation of diversity within normative Judaism.[31]

CLOSING THOUGHTS

At the end of five tractates of the Talmud (*Berakhot, Yevamot, Nazir, Keritot, Tamid*), we find the following teaching: "The disciples of the wise increase peace in the world." When rabbis and scholars are true to their mission, their Torah scholarship is the ideal tool to unite diverse people.

The Talmud celebrates the diversity of the Jewish people by coining a blessing: "Upon seeing a crowd of Israelites, one should say: Blessed is He who discerns secrets (*Barukh Hakham ha-razim*)" (*Berakhot* 58a). Rather than considering conformity to be ideal, the Talmud stresses diversity as something for which God deserves praise. Jewish tradition seeks unity, not conformity.

Although the cliché "two Jews, three opinions" may be true, a more telling adage would be, "one learned Jew, dozens of opinions." The dazzling range of possibilities within Jewish tradition teaches humility and intellectual receptivity; people may hold significantly different opinions and still be united under the roof of the Torah.

Tanakh is the great equalizer in religious education, and should be a model for how we approach all Jewish education. Tanakh educators have the opportunity to bring the wealth of Jewish religious experience and learning into the classroom to teach that multiple voices enrich our understanding of Torah, and that many avenues exist to bring people into an engaged relationship with tradition. The wholeness of the Jewish people is a genuine value at every level.[32]

NOTES

1. Advanced students of Tanakh might consider the subtle distinctions between early medieval approaches of the rabbis of Spain and France. By the thirteenth century with Radak and Ramban, however, commentators began to seamlessly integrate and incorporate the best of both interpretive traditions. Through high school education, the early medieval distinctions generally are not of vital importance to the process of learning Tanakh.

2. "Teaching the 'Wholeness' of the Jewish People," in *Seeking Good, Speaking Peace: Collected Essays of Rabbi Marc D. Angel*, ed. Hayyim Angel (Hoboken, NJ: Ktav, 1994), pp. 255-258. Although this particular excerpt specifically addresses the area of *halakhah*, Rabbi Angel also addresses the broader issue of a comprehensive Jewish education—including Tanakh and history—in his article.

3. Daniel Bouskila, "Rav Uziel's Sephardic Vision for the Jewish People," *Conversations* 29 (Autumn 2017), pp. 111-115.

4. Rabbi Marc D. Angel with Hayyim Angel, *Rabbi Haim David Halevi: Gentle Scholar, Courageous Thinker* (Jerusalem: Urim, 2006), p. 13.

5. For other elements of an idealized Sephardic worldview that focuses on the best values of that world which would benefit all of Jewry, see Rabbi Marc D. Angel, "Models of Sephardic Rabbinic Leadership," *Conversations* 12 (Winter 2012), pp. 171-181; Zvi Zohar, "What All Jews Can Learn from Great Sephardic Rabbis of Recent Centuries," *Conversations* 13 (Spring 2012), pp. 26-38.

6. For an intellectual history of some of the important Sephardic rabbinic thinkers of this period, see Rabbi Marc D. Angel, *Voices in Exile: A Study in Sephardic Intellectual History* (Hoboken, NJ: Ktav, 1991).

7. Rabbi Marc D. Angel, Editor's Introduction, *Conversations* 29 (Autumn 2017), p. vi.

8. From a pure Tanakh interpretation perspective, this approach also remedies a broader educational gap: Most Tanakh scholars and educators ignore the contributions of *all* interpreters from the sixteenth to eighteenth centuries, deeming them inferior to the medieval exegetes and the nineteenth- to twentieth-century commentators. See Amos

Frisch, "A Re-Evaluation of Jewish Biblical Exegesis of the Sixteenth to Nineteenth Centuries" (Hebrew), in *Mehkarim ba-Mikra u-ve-Hinnukh: Studies in Bible and Education Presented to Prof. Moshe Ahrend*, ed. Dov Rappel (Jerusalem: Touro, 1996), pp. 122-141.

9. Quoted in Yehudah Kiel, *Da'at Mikra: Proverbs* (Hebrew), (Jerusalem: Mossad HaRav Kook, 1983), pp. 247-248.

10. Hezekiah was from the Davidic line, and reigned some 200 years after Solomon.

11. Jonathan Jacobs, "The Death of the Child of David from Bathsheba (II Samuel 12:13-25)" (Hebrew), *Megadim* 50 (2009), pp. 135-142.

12. Cited in Rabbi Amnon Bazak, *Shemuel Bet: Malkhut David* (Hebrew), (Jerusalem, Maggid, 2014), pp. 369-370, n. 22.

13. In his book on the Elijah narratives, Rabbi Elhanan Samet draws substantially from the commentaries of Rabbis Laniado and Alsheikh (*Pirkei Eliyahu* [Hebrew], [Maalei Adumim: Maaliyot, 2003]).

14. For discussion of the nature of his work and its contemporary educational relevance, see Ariel Evan Mayse, "*Or haHayyim*: Creativity, Tradition, and Mysticism in the Torah Commentary of R. Hayyim ibn Attar," *Conversations* 13 (Spring 2012), pp. 68-89.

15. Amos Frisch, "On the Interpretive Method of R. Raphael Berdugo (Based on His Exegesis of the Former Prophets)," *Revue des Etudes Juives* 163:3-4 (2004), pp. 445-462.

16. See, for example, Menahem Haran, "Biblical Studies: The Literary Applications of the Numerical Sequence X/X+1 and their Connections with the Patterns of Parallelism" (Hebrew), *Tarbiz* 39 (1970), pp. 122-123; Uriel Simon, *Bakkesh Shalom ve-Rodfehu* (Hebrew), (Tel-Aviv: Yediot Aharonot, 2002), pp. 152-153. Based on his understanding of the poetic parallel, Simon translates the women as saying "Saul and David have killed their thousands, their tens of thousands."

17. Rabbi Elijah Benamozegh, *Israel and Humanity*, trans. Maxwell (Mordechai) Luria (New York: Paulist Press, 1995). See also Luria, "Rabbi Eliyahu Benamozegh: *Israel and Humanity*," *Conversations* 29 (Autumn 2017), pp. 101-110; Clemence Boulouque, "An 'Interior Occident' and the Case for an Oriental Modernity: The Livornese

Printing Press and the Mediterranean Publishing Networks of Elia Benamozegh," *Jewish Social Studies* 23:2 (Winter 2018), pp. 86-136, esp. pp. 91-93.

18. For an overview of several central themes in the *Me'am Lo'ez*, see Rabbi Marc D. Angel, *Voices in Exile: A Study in Sephardic Intellectual History* (Hoboken, NJ: Ktav, 1991), pp. 103-110.

19. I am particularly grateful to Rabbi Meir Abitbol and Rabbi Yitzhak Chouraqi for helping me create this list. Thank you also to Rabbi Ilan Acoca, Rabbi Marc D. Angel, Rabbi Richard Hidary, Hakham Isaac Sassoon, Professor Daniel Tsadik, and Professor Zvi Zohar for their assistance. For a remarkable array of Sephardic commentaries and other works, see http://www.wslibrary.net/sifria/en/12-books.

20. For a summary, see Hayyim Angel, "Transitions and Expansions within Psalms," in *Vision from the Prophet and Counsel from the Elders: A Survey of Nevi'im and Ketuvim* (New York: OU Press, 2013), pp. 223-225.

21. Another excellent example of appending a discussion of liturgical customs to an analysis of a psalm may be found in Rabbi Elhanan Samet's classes 1-5 on Psalm 100, at https://www.etzion.org.il/en/topics/tehillim-advanced-series-2 (accessed May 21, 2019).

22. Rabbi Shalom Carmy, "'I Will Bless God at All Times': *Pesukei De-Zimrah* on Shabbat and on Weekdays," in *MiTokh Ha-Ohel, From Within the Tent: The Shabbat Prayers*, ed. Daniel Z. Feldman and Stuart W. Halpern (Jerusalem: Maggid, 2015), pp. 143–149.

23. Macy Nulman, *The Encyclopedia of Jewish Prayer: Ashkenazic and Sephardic Rites* (Northvale, NJ: Jason Aronson, 1993), p. 327.

24. Rabbi Elhanan Samet, *Pirkei Elisha* (Hebrew), (Ma'alei Adumim: Ma'aliyot, 2007), pp. 281–284.

25. The severity of this prophetic passage gave rise to an ancient debate over its appropriateness as a *haftarah*. In *Megillah* 25a-b, Rabbi Eleazar specifically rails against using this passage as a *haftarah*: "Rabbi Eleazar says: 'Make known to Jerusalem' (Ezekiel 16) is not read as a *haftarah*." The Talmud (25b): "On one occasion a man read in the presence of Rabbi Eleazar 'Make known to Jerusalem her abominations.' He said to him, 'While you are investigating the abominations of Jerusalem, go

and investigate the abominations of your own mother.' Inquiries were made into his birth, and he was found to be illegitimate." Following the majority opinion against R. Eleazar, Rambam (*Seder Tefillot le-Khol ha-Shanah*) adopts Ezekiel 16 as the *haftarah* of *Shemot*, and the Yemenite tradition follows his ruling.

26. For further discussion of this issue and the vital necessity of educators teaching both customs as valid and sacred, see Rabbi Marc D. Angel, "*Minhagim*: Divinity and Diversity," *Conversations* 29 (Autumn 2017), pp. 11-12.

27. Some of Gra's students who subsequently moved to Israel realized their master's dream and reinstated the daily recital, resulting in the contemporary practice that many Ashkenazic communities in Israel recite the Priestly Blessing daily.

28. See further discussion of this issue in Rabbi Daniel Sperber, "Daily *Birkat Kohanim* in the Diaspora," *Conversations* 20 (Autumn 2014), pp. 150-155. Sperber supports the view that all communities should recite the Priestly Blessing on a daily (or at least weekly) basis.

29. Elhanan Samet, *Iyyunim be-Parashot ha-Shavua* (third series), vol. 2 (Hebrew) ed. Ayal Fishler (Tel-Aviv: Yediot Aharonot, 2012), pp. 190-217.

30. For broader educational discussions of this issue, see Rabbi Marc D. Angel, "*Minhagim*: Divinity and Diversity," *Conversations* 29 (Autumn 2017), pp. 3-18; Rabbi Ariel Cohen, "Ashkenazim and Sephardim— United in Education," *Conversations* 29 (Autumn 2017), pp. 19-24.

31. See further discussion of liturgical differences in Hayyim Angel, "A Study of Sephardic and Ashkenazic Liturgy," in *Increasing Peace Through Balanced Torah Study. Conversations* 27 (New York: Institute for Jewish Ideas and Ideals, 2017), pp. 30-37.

32. See further discussion in Hayyim Angel, "'The Disciples of the Wise Increase Peace in the World': The Use of Traditional Scholarship to Build Bridges and Mend Rifts," *Conversations* 26 (Autumn 2016), pp. 20-32.

WHERE THE RULES OF *PESHAT* AND *PESAK* COLLIDE:

DEUTERONOMY AND PROPHETIC NARRATIVES[*]

INTRODUCTION

To a large degree, Tanakh and *halakhah* operate on different planes. Biblical commentators concern themselves with the meaning of Tanakh, whereas legal decisors work primarily with the Talmud and later authoritative halakhic codes and rulings. In *halakhah*, talmudic passages are intended as literal and are generally accepted as binding by later rabbinic authorities. In *aggadah*, talmudic passages often are intended as allegorical. Even when they are understood literally, later commentators generally reserve the right to disagree with them.[1]

This distinction is self-evident to Rabbi Yom Tov Lipmann Heller (1579–1654), who extends the argument to the arena of theoretical *halakhah*, that is, situations when there are no practical consequences (I have added several clarifying points in brackets):

> Rambam wrote… even though the Gemara did not interpret [the Mishnah] in that manner. Since there is no practical legal difference, permission is granted to interpret [the Mishnah in a manner different from the Gemara's interpretation]. I see no difference between interpreting Mishnah and interpreting Scripture. Regarding Scripture, permission is granted to interpret

---

[*]   This essay appeared originally in Hayyim Angel, *Creating Space between Peshat and Derash* (Jersey City, NJ: Ktav, 2011), pp. 52-63.

[differently from how the Gemara interprets] as our own eyes see in the commentaries written since the time of the Gemara. However, we must not make any halakhic ruling that contradicts the Gemara (*Tosafot Yom Tov* commentary on *Nazir* 5:5).

There are occasions, however, where halakhic rulings are based primarily on *peshat* readings of biblical verses outside of the Torah, rather than on normative rabbinic halakhic texts. This difference creates the unusual situation where *pashtanim* may clash with halakhists on *peshat* grounds. This essay will consider three such occasions as a means of exploring different aspects of the conflict between the two sets of rules.

THE TEST OF A FALSE PROPHET

And should you ask yourselves, "How can we know that the oracle was not spoken by the Lord?"—if the prophet speaks in the name of the Lord and the oracle does not come true, that oracle was not spoken by the Lord; the prophet has uttered it presumptuously: do not stand in dread of him (Deuteronomy 18:21–22).

There does not appear to be any ambiguity in this law. Anyone claiming prophecy whose predictions fail to come true must be a false prophet and is executed in court.

However, these verses are not easily taken at face value. Jonah and Isaiah both were true prophets. Nevertheless, Jonah's prediction of the destruction of Nineveh did not occur (Jonah 3:4–10), nor did Isaiah's prediction of Hezekiah's imminent death (II Kings 20:1–11~Isaiah 38:1–8). In both instances, repentance warded off the negative decrees.

Rambam turns to the Book of Jeremiah for clarification. During his conflict with the false prophet Hananiah son of Azzur, Jeremiah stated:

> The prophets who lived before you and me from ancient times prophesied war, disaster, and pestilence against many lands and great kingdoms. So if a prophet prophesies good fortune, then only when the word of the prophet comes true can it be known that the Lord really sent him (Jeremiah 28:8–9).

Rambam understands Jeremiah's challenge to Hananiah as a modification of Deuteronomy 18:21–22. He therefore rules that if one prophesies something negative, the decree can be abrogated by repentance. However, if one prophesies something positive, the prediction must come true in full or else the person is executed as a false prophet:

> Regarding prophecies of doom… if they do not occur, his prophetic standing is not contradicted… it is possible that they repented and God forgave them as in the case of the people of Nineveh; or that retribution was deferred as in the case of Hezekiah. However, if he promised that good would occur… and it did not, then it is known for certain that he is a false prophet. Any good decree from God, even if it is provisional, is not retracted…as we learn in Tractate *Shabbat* (55a). We learn from this principle that a prophet may be tested only through his positive prophecies. This is what Jeremiah told Hananiah son of Azzur (Rambam, *Hilkhot Yesodei ha-Torah* 10:4).[2]

From the perspective of Jeremiah's audience, the sudden downfall of Babylonia was indeed a favorable prophecy. Thus, were Babylonia not to fall in two years as Hananiah had predicted, Hananiah certainly would be a false prophet. On the other hand, if Babylonia were to fall after two years, Jeremiah could not be convicted as a false prophet since he would be able to claim that the people repented and therefore averted the decree of destruction he had been proclaiming.

Abarbanel challenges Rambam's reading of Jeremiah 28:8–9. Without going into the technical points here, the different interpretations may be summarized in this manner:

"You know the prophets who lived in the past and prophesied doom?"

Rambam: "It was only when one of them would prophesy good fortune and the prophecy came true that it would be known for sure that the Lord really sent him."

Abarbanel: "When a prophet would prophesy good fortune in opposition to those prophets of the past, only if the prophecy came true would it be known for sure that the Lord really sent him."

Abarbanel views Hananiah as vulnerable because of his opposition to a long prophetic tradition, not because he made a positive prediction.

Aside from Abarbanel's objections to Rambam's reading of Jeremiah 28:8–9, other verses in Jeremiah appear to contradict Rambam's ruling outright:

At one moment I may decree that a nation or a kingdom shall be uprooted and pulled down and destroyed; but if that nation against which I made the decree turns back from its wickedness, I change My mind concerning the punishment I planned to bring on it. At another moment I may decree that a nation or a kingdom shall be built and planted; but if

it does what is displeasing to Me and does not obey Me, then
I change My mind concerning the good I planned to bestow
upon it (Jeremiah 18:7–10).

This passage suggests that *all* prophecies are contingent on human
behavior. If people repent after a negative prophecy, the decree may
be annulled. Conversely, if people do evil, a favorable prophecy may
be repealed. Not only does this passage challenge Rambam's ruling,
but it appears to be antithetical to Deuteronomy 18:21–22. The
Torah indicates that all prophetic predictions must occur or else
one may be executed as a false prophet. Jeremiah 18:7–10 indicates
that all prophecies are contingent on the behavior of an individual
or nation and therefore the outcomes may not match the predictions.

Rambam addresses this conflict in chapter 2 of his *Introduction to the
Commentary of the Mishnah*. Jeremiah 28 is generally correct. When a
prophet announces evil tidings and they do not occur, we may assume
that the people repented and God forgave them. If, however, a prophet
predicts something positive, then his prediction must occur to verify
him as a prophet. Jeremiah 18, on the other hand, discusses only cases
where the prophet never announced the good tidings in public; such
positive prophecies are vulnerable to changes in behavior. Rambam
cites Jacob as an example: he feared that his sins might have cancelled
the good future which God had privately promised him.[3]

Ralbag, Rabbi Yitzhak Arama, and Abarbanel challenge Rambam,
deeming it unlikely that God would keep His word when the prophet
announced the prophecy in public, whereas He would be willing to
retract a good decree if nobody else knew of it. Further, Jeremiah
18:7–10 does not distinguish between public and private prophecies.

Rabbi Yitzhak Arama (*Akedat Yitzhak, sha'ar* 96) asserts that prophecy generally is contingent on consistent behavior by the recipients as per Jeremiah 18. Deuteronomy 18:21–22 deals only with the limited case where two unproven prophets present conflicting predictions—as in the case of Jeremiah vs. Hananiah. In such instances, how could people determine which one is telling the truth? The answer is that whichever one of those prophecies is not fulfilled is false.[4]

To summarize: Rambam rules that if a prophet predicts a good occurrence and it does not come true in entirety, we would execute the prophet in court. According to Ralbag, Rabbi Yitzhak Arama, and Abarbanel, we would not execute him, since it is possible that the negative behavior of an individual or nation would have abrogated, mitigated, or delayed the fulfillment of that prediction. There are no halakhic sources in Talmud or midrash that govern this case. These halakhic positions are rooted in a *peshat* debate over how best to reconcile Deuteronomy 18:21–22 with Jeremiah 18:7–10 and 28:8–9.

According to the rules of learning *peshat* in Tanakh, this is a debate among rabbinic commentators, and their different views must be evaluated against the textual evidence. According to the rules of *pesak*, however, not all commentators are equal. Were this halakhic possibility to exist today, would Rambam carry more weight because he was a great halakhist, whereas the others were not in his league? Or should a *posek* learn the verses and at least possibly decide that the reading of Ralbag, Rabbi Yitzhak Arama, and Abarbanel is more likely and therefore not execute someone who prophesies something positive that does not occur?

MONARCHY

If, after you have entered the land that the Lord your God has assigned to you, and taken possession of it and settled in it, you decide, "I will set a king over me, as do all the nations about

me," you shall be free to set a king over yourself, one chosen
by the Lord your God. Be sure to set as king over yourself one
of your own people; you must not set a foreigner over you, one
who is not your kinsman (Deuteronomy 17:14–15).

Samuel was displeased that they said, "Give us a king to govern us." Samuel prayed to the Lord, and the Lord replied to
Samuel, "Heed the demand of the people in everything they
say to you. For it is not you that they have rejected; it is Me
they have rejected as their king" (I Samuel 8:6–7).

Surprisingly, the Torah's formulation legislates monarchy only
in the second verse of the passage. This, coupled with Samuel's
vigorous opposition to the people's request, led to a talmudic debate
whether the Torah commands monarchy or whether it permits and
governs it when the people request a king. Rabbi Yehudah (*Sanhedrin*
20b) considers monarchy a positive commandment. Rabbi Nehorai
maintains that it is permitted yet frowned upon. In *Sifrei Devarim*
156, Rabbi Nehorai asserts that monarchy is shameful for Israel.
He cites I Samuel 8:7, where God deems the people's request to be
a rejection of divine rule. Rabbi Yehudah retorts that monarchy is
a commandment but that the people sinned in Samuel's time by
requesting a king inappropriately.

Rambam rules like Rabbi Yehudah, that monarchy is a positive
commandment and that Samuel opposed the manner in which the
people asked for a king (*Hilkhot Melakhim* 1:1–2). Many later commentators and codifiers adopted this position.

In his commentary on Deuteronomy and Samuel, Abarbanel
offers a thorough critique of Rambam's view. God and Samuel were
incensed at the people's very asking for a king, rather than at the
specific formulation or timing of their request (cf. I Samuel 10:19;

12:19). If the Torah commands monarchy, why did Joshua and his successors fail to appoint a king? When Samuel rebuked the people, why did they not respond that they simply wanted to fulfill a Torah commandment?

Abarbanel therefore adopts Rabbi Nehorai's view that while the Torah permits monarchy if requested, the institution is fundamentally negative. Abarbanel likens monarchy to the laws of the "beautiful captive" (Deuteronomy 21:10–14) as another case where the Torah permits certain less-than-ideal actions to forestall worse eventualities (cf. *Kiddushin* 21b).

To summarize: in this instance, the Talmud and halakhic midrashim present an unresolved disagreement over how to reconcile the biblical verses. Rambam and Abarbanel take opposite sides of this debate at least partially, if not primarily, as a result of their analysis of *peshat* in the biblical verses.

Again we may ask: were this halakhic possibility to exist today, would Rambam carry more weight because he was a great halakhist, while Abarbanel was not at that level? Or should a *posek* learn the verse and at least possibly decide that Abarbanel's reading is more likely and therefore not insist on a monarchy if people do not want one?

Although we do not have actual monarchy today, the laws of monarchy in the Torah form the basis of many contemporary discussions regarding the halakhic authority of the elected government of the State of Israel. In an Orthodox Forum volume, Rabbi Aharon Lichtenstein and Professor Gerald Blidstein discuss monarchy as a precedent for the authority of Israel's civil government. Writing as a halakhist, Rabbi Lichtenstein quotes Ibn Ezra (who also believes that monarchy is permitted and not commanded) and Abarbanel alongside Rambam, but he adds the caveat that they are "admittedly of far lesser status as *baalei halakhah* [halakhic authorities]." Surveying Jewish thought, Professor Blidstein cites all three equally as prominent medieval rabbinic authorities on the subject.[5]

SOLOMON'S MARRIAGE TO AN EGYPTIAN WOMAN

You shall not abhor an Edomite, for he is your kinsman. You shall not abhor an Egyptian, for you were a stranger in his land. Children born to them may be admitted into the congregation of the Lord in the third generation (Deuteronomy 23:8–9).

Solomon allied himself by marriage with Pharaoh king of Egypt. He married Pharaoh's daughter and brought her to the City of David [to live there] until he had finished building his palace, and the House of the Lord, and the walls around Jerusalem. The people, however, continued to offer sacrifices at the open shrines, because up to that time no house had been built for the name of the Lord. And Solomon, though he loved the Lord and followed the practices of his father David, also sacrificed and offered at the shrines (I Kings 3:1–3).

In the two aforementioned cases, medieval rabbis debated halakhic issues. While Rambam is a classical halakhic decisor whereas Ibn Ezra, Ralbag, Rabbi Yitzhak Arama, and Abarbanel are not, nobody disputed a final talmudic legal ruling. In the case of Solomon's marriage to Pharaoh's daughter, however, a final talmudic legal ruling is at stake.

There is a debate in a Mishnah (*Yevamot* 76b) whether Egyptian women are included in the Torah's prohibition against Egyptians in Deuteronomy 23:8–9. The majority view prohibits both men and women until the third generation after they convert, while Rabbi Shimon permits Egyptian women who convert to marry Israelites immediately. Although Rabbi Shimon claims a received tradition, the Talmud rules like the majority opinion.

Despite this clear talmudic ruling, however, Radak and Abarbanel puzzle over the fact that the Book of Kings does not condemn Solomon for marrying Pharaoh's daughter, reserving its criticism for when his wives led his heart astray at the end of his life (I Kings 11). According to the talmudic ruling, however, Solomon was guilty of violating the Torah's prohibition against intermarriage with an Egyptian, even if she had converted beforehand.

Radak suggests that the neutral tone of the Kings narrative in chapter 3 indicates that in fact Rabbi Shimon's rejected view must have been in force in Solomon's time, that is, that Egyptian women were permitted to convert and marry Israelites:

> In truth, it appears that [Solomon] converted her to the Jewish religion[6] even though she was prohibited to him as a first- generation Egyptian. There was a Sage who believed that she was permitted to him.... And even though the law is not like this Sage despite his claim of a received tradition, his ruling appears correct. We do not find in the verses condemnation of Solomon for marrying Pharaoh's daughter (Radak on I Kings 3:3).

The talmudic ruling is purely theoretical, since the halakhic category of "Egyptian" prohibited by the Torah no longer exists today. Therefore, Radak is arguing over historical circumstances rather than disputing a ruling of the Talmud that has practical ramifications. What Radak would think if there were halakhic Egyptians today is a matter of speculation, but it lies at the heart of this conflict between the sets of rules governing *peshat* and *pesak*.[7]

In his analysis of the Kings passage, Abarbanel first proposes several hypothetical alternative readings of Deuteronomy 23:8–9:

166

(1) Perhaps being "admitted into the congregation" does not refer to marriage, as is commonly assumed. (2) Perhaps, as per Rabbi Shimon and Radak, Egyptian women were excluded from the prohibition. (3) Perhaps the Torah intended this law to apply exclusively to the first three generations of Egyptians from the time of the exodus, since only they enslaved the Israelites. After that initial prohibition, however, Egyptians who converted could marry Israelites immediately.

After those theoretical suggestions, however, Abarbanel submits to the halakhic understanding of the verse: that it does apply to marriage to Egyptians even in Solomon's time, and the prohibition includes Egyptian women as well as men. Confronted by what he perceives as an irresolvable tension, Abarbanel concludes that Solomon erred in his understanding of Torah law. He was young and it was good diplomacy to marry the Egyptian princess, so God did not punish or even criticize him for the marriage. Unlike Radak, Abarbanel resigns himself to reconciling the perspectives of *peshat* and *pesak* in this instance, leading him to the remarkable conclusion that Solomon was ignorant of the *halakhah* governing his marriage.

To summarize: although the Talmud reached a halakhic ruling in this instance, Radak believes that the rejected minority opinion in fact is historically correct based on his reading of the Book of Kings. While initially entertaining several *peshat* alternatives, Abarbanel ultimately resigns himself to the authoritative halakhic ruling of the Talmud and explains the biblical text in its light.

CONCLUSION

In the case of ascertaining false prophets, Rambam bases a halakhic ruling on a *peshat* analysis of the apparent conflicts between Deuteronomy 18:21–22, Jeremiah 18:7–10, and Jeremiah 28:8–9.

Several *pashtanim* challenge Rambam's reading of those biblical texts and with it his ruling on a capital case. Similarly, Rambam's halakhic ruling on the institution of monarchy is rooted at least partially in *peshat* readings of the apparent conflict between the laws in Deuteronomy 17:14–15 and the narratives in I Samuel 8–12. Abarbanel challenges Rambam's reading of *peshat* and with it his halakhic decision. In a third instance, Radak and Abarbanel confront the talmudic ruling that female Egyptians as well as their male counterparts cannot marry Israelites even after conversion (based on Deuteronomy 23:8–9). However, they wonder if that ruling in fact was practiced in Solomon's time, given that the Book of Kings does not criticize Solomon's marriage to Pharaoh's daughter (I Kings 3:1–3).

These fascinating tensions are inherent to the system. It is important to recognize how each set of rules can yield different results within a traditional learning framework.

NOTES

1. See, e.g., Rabbi Marc D. Angel, "Authority and Dissent: A Discussion of Boundaries," *Tradition* 25:2 (Winter 1990), pp. 18–27; Rabbi Hayyim David Halevi, *Aseh Lekha Rav*, vol. 5, resp. #49 (pp. 304–307); Rabbi Michael Rosensweig, "*Elu va-Elu Divre Elokim Hayyim*: Halakhic Pluralism and Theories of Controversy," *Tradition* 26:3 (Spring 1992), pp. 4–23; Marc Saperstein, *Decoding the Rabbis: A Thirteenth-Century Commentary on the Aggadah* (Cambridge MA: Harvard University Press, 1980), pp. 1–20.

2. Translation (with minor modifications) from Eliyahu Touger, *Mishneh Torah* (NY-Jerusalem: Moznaim Publishing, 1989). Cf. JT *Sanhedrin* 11:5.

3. See Genesis 28:15, where God promised Jacob that He will protect him wherever he goes, and 32:8, where Jacob was frightened nevertheless. Cf. *Berakhot* 4a.

4. According to this line of interpretation, however, one must wonder whether if there were such a prophetic conflict, would God insist on proving the true prophet's veracity even if people were to change their behavior. In our case, for example, were the people to have repented fully, would God have allowed the Babylonians to destroy Jerusalem and the Temple simply to prove Jeremiah right?

5. Rabbi Aharon Lichtenstein, "Communal Governance, Lay and Rabbinic: An Overview," pp. 19–52, esp. pp. 21–26; Gerald Blidstein, "On Lay Legislation in Halakhah: The King as Instance," pp. 1–17, in *Rabbinic and Lay Communal Authority*, ed. Suzanne Last Stone (New York: Yeshiva University Press, 2006).

6. Cf. Rambam, *Hilkhot Issurei Bi'ah* 13:14, who also assumes that King Solomon must have converted Pharaoh's daughter before marrying her.

7. For a broader discussion of Radak's approach to conflicts between *peshat* and halakhic rulings of the Talmud, see Naomi Grunhaus, "'*Ve-Af Al Pi she-Razal Kibbelu*': Peshat and Halakhah in Radak's Exegesis, in *Between Rashi and Maimonides: Themes in Medieval Jewish Thought, Literature and Exegesis*, ed. Ephraim Kanarfogel and Moshe Sokolow (New York: Yeshiva University Press, 2010), pp. 343-364.

HUR AND
PHARAOH'S DAUGHTER:

MIDRASHIC READINGS OF SILENT HEROES*

INTRODUCTION

An ever-present struggle within religious Tanakh interpretation relates to the degree of our reliance on the talmudic Sages and post-talmudic rabbinic commentators for guidance. They were truly exceptional religious scholars who viewed the biblical text as the revealed word of God, and therefore they serve as our ultimate teachers. Simultaneously, we must consider them as our guides and teachers rather than as substitutes for the text.[1] We try our utmost to learn Tanakh in the manner that our *mefarshim* (commentators) did. We need our *mefarshim* to teach us how to learn and think, but we also need to distinguish between text and interpretation.

Much has been written to define the term *peshat*, and I prefer the working definition that *peshat* is the primary message the author intended to convey to the reader.[2] Our goal is to allow the prophetic words in Tanakh to transform us, rather than to impose our logic and values onto the text. In *halakhah*, talmudic passages are intended as literal and generally accepted as binding.[3] In *aggadah*, talmudic passages often are intended as allegorical. Even when these passages

---

* This essay appeared originally in *Mitokh Ha-Ohel: Essays on the Weekly Parashah from the Rabbis and Professors of Yeshiva University*, ed. Daniel Z. Feldman and Stuart W. Halpern (New York: Yeshiva University Press, 2010), pp. 205-213.

are understood literally, later commentators reserve the right to disagree with them.[4] This distinction is self-evident to Rabbi Yom Tov Lipmann Heller (1579–1654), author of the *Tosafot Yom Tov* commentary on the Mishnah, who extends the argument to the arena of theoretical *halakhah*, that is, when there are no practical consequences. After observing that Rambam's reading of a halakhic Mishnah differs from that of the Gemara, Rabbi Heller explains why Rambam feels free to disagree with the Talmud even in halakhic matters (I have added several clarifying points in brackets):

> Since there is no practical legal difference, permission is granted to interpret [the Mishnah in a manner different from the Gemara's interpretation]. I see no difference between interpreting Mishnah and interpreting Scripture. Regarding Scripture, permission is granted to interpret [differently from how the Gemara interprets] as our own eyes see in the commentaries written since the time of the Gemara. However, we must not make any halakhic ruling that contradicts the Gemara (commentary on Mishnah *Nazir* 5:5).

Some within the Orthodox world adopt only half of that truth at the expense of the other. One side dogmatically adopts talmudic and midrashic teachings as literal, and insists that this position is required as part of having faith in the teachings of the Sages. Another group dismisses the talmudic traditions as being far removed from biblical text and reality. The first group accuses the second of denigration of the Sages, whereas the second group accuses the first of being fundamentalists who ignore science and scholarship.

The truth is, this rift has been around for a long time. In the twelfth century, Rambam lamented this very imbalance his introduction to *Perek Helek* in Tractate *Sanhedrin*. He divided Jews into three categories. The first group piously accepts all rabbinic teachings as literal:

> The first group is the largest one…. They understand the
> teachings of the Sages only in their literal sense, in spite of the
> fact that some of their teachings, when taken literally, seem so
> fantastic and irrational that if one were to repeat them literally, even to the uneducated, let alone sophisticated scholars,
> their amazement would prompt them to ask how anyone in
> the world could believe such things true, much less edifying.
> The members of this group are poor in knowledge. One can
> only regret their folly. Their very effort to honor and to exalt
> the Sages in accordance with their own meager understanding
> actually humiliates them. As God lives, this group destroys
> the glory of the Torah of God and says the opposite of what it
> intended. For He said in His perfect Torah, "The nation is a
> wise and understanding people" (Deuteronomy 4:6).

Such individuals are pious but foolish. They misunderstand the
intent of the Sages and draw false conclusions in the name of religion.
Misguided as this first group is, it is preferable to the second
group, which also takes the words of the Sages literally but rejects
their teachings as a result:

> The second group is also a numerous one. It, too, consists of
> persons who, having read or heard the words of the Sages, understand them according to their simple literal sense and believe that
> the Sages intended nothing else than what may be learned from
> their literal interpretation. Inevitably, they ultimately declare the
> Sages to be fools, hold them up to contempt, and slander what
> does not deserve to be slandered…. The members of this group

are so pretentiously stupid that they can never attain genuine
wisdom.... This is an accursed group, because they attempt to
refute men of established greatness whose wisdom has been
demonstrated to competent men of science.

The first group is reverent to the Sages, whereas the second group
is open to science and scholarship but rejects the Sages and their
teachings. Both groups fail because of their fundamental misunderstanding of the Sages.

Rambam then celebrates that rare ideal scholar, who combines
those two half truths into the whole truth:

> There is a third group. Its members are so few in number that
> it is hardly appropriate to call them a group.... This group
> consists of men to whom the greatness of our Sages is clear....
> They know that the Sages did not speak nonsense, and it is
> clear to them that the words of the Sages contain both an
> obvious and a hidden meaning. Thus, whenever the Sages
> spoke of things that seem impossible, they were employing
> the style of riddle and parable which is the method of truly
> great thinkers.[5]

In addition to Rambam's insistence on the fact that the Sages did
not always mean their words literally, we must add that the greatest
peshat commentators, from Rabbi Saadiah Gaon to Rashi to Ibn Ezra
to Ramban to Abarbanel and so many others, venerated the Sages
without being bound by their non-legal comments. These rabbinic
thinkers combine reverence for the Sages with a commitment to
scholarship and integrity to the text of the Torah.[6]

In this essay, we will use this methodology to explore midrashic
readings of two minor characters in the Torah: Hur and Pharaoh's

173

daughter. Midrashim carefully weave together the biblical evidence to create fuller personalities.

HUR

From the beginning of Moses' tenure as Israel's leader, three people stood by his side: his brother Aaron, his disciple Joshua, and Hur. Who was Hur? Since the Torah provides only scant evidence, Ibn Ezra aptly remarks that "we do not know who he is" (short commentary on Exodus 24:14).

First, let us consider the explicit references to Hur in the Torah. During Israel's battle against Amalek, Moses ordered Joshua to lead the troops. Moses, Aaron, and Hur ascended the hill, and Aaron and Hur supported Moses' tiring arms:

> Joshua did as Moses told him and fought with Amalek, while Moses, Aaron, and Hur went up to the top of the hill. Then, whenever Moses held up his hand, Israel prevailed; but whenever he let down his hand, Amalek prevailed. But Moses' hands grew heavy; so they took a stone and put it under him and he sat on it, while Aaron and Hur, one on each side, supported his hands; thus his hands remained steady until the sun set (Exodus 17:10–12).

Hur never is given a "proper" introduction but clearly is among the highest echelons of the nation's leadership.

This impression is confirmed as Moses ascended Mount Sinai to receive the Torah. Again, his three associates occupied important positions. Moses' disciple Joshua waited for his master at the base of the mountain while Moses delegated the national leadership to Aaron and Hur:

So Moses and his attendant Joshua arose, and Moses ascended the mountain of God. To the elders he had said, "Wait here for us until we return to you. You have Aaron and Hur with you; let anyone who has a legal matter approach them" (Exodus 24:13-14).

It is surprising, then, that when the people despaired of Moses' return from Sinai they clamored only to Aaron and built the Golden Calf:

When the people saw that Moses was so long in coming down from the mountain, the people gathered against Aaron and said to him, "Come, make us a god who shall go before us, for that man Moses, who brought us from the land of Egypt—we do not know what has happened to him" (Exodus 32:1).

Similarly, Moses found Joshua at the base of the mountain, right where he had been waiting (Exodus 32:17–18). Mysteriously, though, Hur disappears from the narrative, and we never hear about him again. Where did he go? On the textual level, we never will know.

We are left to the world of midrash, which capitalizes on any information it can glean from Tanakh. The portrait of Hur may be developed in different layers.

[When the people wanted to build the Golden Calf,] Hur arose and rebuked them, "You brainless fools! Have you forgotten the miracles God performed for you?" Whereupon they rose against him and killed him. They then came to Aaron… and said to him: "We will do to you what we have done to this man." When Aaron saw the state of affairs, he was afraid (*Exodus Rabbah* 41:7).

This midrash casts Hur as a religious martyr. His sudden disappearance in the text lends itself to this interpretation.[7] This reading also helps explain Aaron's surprising willingness to build the Calf, and also provides *someone* in the camp who opposed the Calf while Moses was atop the mountain.

The next layer of Hur's midrashic portrait derives from the construction of the Tabernacle. God designated Bezalel as the chief artisan in the construction:

> See, I have singled out by name Bezalel son of Uri son of Hur, of the tribe of Judah (Exodus 31:2).

Why would the Torah trace Bezalel back to his grandfather Hur? One midrash states that since Hur martyred himself during the Calf episode, God rewarded him by choosing his grandson Bezalel as the chief artisan:

> Why is Hur mentioned here? Because when Israel were about to serve idols, he jeopardized his life on God's behalf and would not allow them to do so, with the result that they slew him. Whereupon the Holy One, blessed be He, said: I assure you that I will repay you for this (*Exodus Rabbah* 48:3).[8]

At the level of *peshat*, God chose Bezalel because Bezalel was a gifted artist. This midrashic expansion highlights his descent from Hur. Hur had heroically opposed the Golden Calf, and now Hur's grandson would build the Tabernacle—the antithesis of the Golden Calf.

In Chronicles, the Sages found another clue to Hur's personality. In the genealogy of the tribe of Judah, Caleb son of Hezron married Ephrath, who gave birth to Hur:

> When Azubah died, Caleb married Ephrath, who bore him Hur. Hur begot Uri, and Uri begot Bezalel (I Chronicles 2:19–20).

Whether this Caleb son of Hezron (a son of Perez son of Judah) should be identified with Caleb son of Jephunneh on the level of *peshat* is dubious (see Ibn Ezra's short commentary on Exodus 24:14). However, several midrashim identify them at the level of *derash*. Caleb son of Jephunneh was the most heroic spy during that disaster, stalwartly opposing his colleagues and the entire nation and demanding that they have faith in God. The nation threatened to stone him (Numbers 13:30; 14:6–10). Perhaps the midrashim that depict Hur's heroic martyrdom during the Calf episode derive in part from the story of Caleb. By creating this conceptual father-son relationship, the midrashic story of Hur's martyrdom becomes even more poignant. Caleb and Hur are cast as the two courageous men of faith who opposed everyone else during Israel's two greatest sins in the wilderness. Caleb was almost killed by the mob in *peshat*, whereas Hur was killed by the mob in *derash*.

One final layer of *derash* interpretation emerges from the midrashic identification of Ephrath, Hur's mother (from I Chronicles 2:19–20), with Miriam:

> The king of Egypt spoke to the Hebrew midwives (Exodus 1:15): Rav and Shemuel [differ in their interpretation]; one said they were… Jochebed and Miriam; and [the other said] they were Jochebed and Elisheba (Aaron's wife, see Exodus 6:23)….

> And because the midwives feared God, He established households for them (Exodus 1:21): Rav and Shemuel [differ in their interpretation]; one said they are the priestly and Levitical houses, and the other said they are the royal houses. One who says they are the priestly and Levitical houses: Aaron and Moses; and one who says they are the royal houses: for also David descended from Miriam, as it is written: When

177

Azubah died, Caleb married Ephrath, who bore him Hur. Hur begot Uri, and Uri begot Bezalel (I Chronicles 2:19), and it is written: Now David was the son of that Ephrathite etc. (I Samuel 17:12) (*Sotah* 11b).

In the Torah, Miriam watched over baby Moses' ark. The associations of the midwives Shiphrah and Puah with Jochebed and Miriam (or Elisheba) in this talmudic passage further underscore the midrashic characterization of Miriam as a risk-taker as she heroically defied Pharaoh's murderous decrees.

By having Hur's midrashic parents as Caleb son of Jephunneh and Miriam, Hur's background is fleshed out. Both his parents put their lives on the line for God and their people. As a bonus, these associations would make Hur into Moses' nephew. The two individuals supporting Moses' tired arms in the battle against Amalek would be Moses' brother in *peshat* and his sister's son in *derash*.

The texts in Exodus and Chronicles give us precious few hints to Hur's character, despite his being so prominent a leader at the time of the Exodus. At the level of *peshat*, Hur was from the tribe of Judah (I Chronicles 2:19–20) and likely was the grandfather of the artisan Bezalel (Exodus 31:2). The various midrashim we have considered expand him into a religious hero and martyr, son of two of the elite members of the desert generation: Caleb and Miriam. Hur thereby is brought to life through these midrashic expansions.

PHARAOH'S DAUGHTER

The daughter of Pharaoh came down to bathe in the Nile, while her maidens walked along the Nile. She spied the basket among the reeds and sent her slave girl to fetch it. When she opened it, she saw that it was a child, a boy crying. She took pity on it and said, "This must be a Hebrew child." Then his sister said to Pharaoh's daughter, "Shall I go and get you a Hebrew nurse to suckle the child for you?" And Pharaoh's daughter answered, "Yes." So the girl went and called the child's mother. And Pharaoh's daughter said to her, "Take this child and nurse it for me, and I will pay your wages." So the woman took the child and nursed it. When the child grew up, she brought him to Pharaoh's daughter, who made him her son. She named him Moses, explaining, "I drew him out of the water" (Exodus 2:5–10).

The story of Pharaoh's daughter is relatively straightforward in *peshat*. Pharaoh's daughter knew Moses was an Israelite, either because he was circumcised or because mothers do not normally float their babies down a river. There also is something delightfully ironic about Miriam's getting Pharaoh's daughter to pay Moses' mother Jochebed to nurse Moses.

Perhaps the most curious element in the *peshat* is that Pharaoh's daughter names the baby "Moses," since "I drew him out of the water" (*ki min ha-mayim meshitihu*). How did Pharaoh's daughter know sufficient Hebrew to make such a wordplay? Hizkuni and Abarbanel were so bothered by this question that they espoused a forced reading that Moses' mother named him. A more likely interpretation, adopted by Shadal and Netziv, is that "Moses" was an Egyptian name, meaning "son." "I drew him out of the water" explains why she adopted him, not why she named him Moshe. The Torah then makes a Hebrew wordplay when translating her rationale. At the level of *peshat*, then, Pharaoh's daughter serves as an agent of Moses' rescue and adoptive mother and then disappears from the narrative.

Some midrashim, however, exploit several details in this brief account that would not have bearing in *peshat*. For example, one midrash asks why Pharaoh's daughter would go to the river to bathe. Were there no baths in the palace? The midrash answers: Pharaoh's daughter was using the river as a *mikveh* in order to banish paganism from herself, essentially converting to Judaism (*Sotah* 12a; cf. *Exodus Rabbah* 1:23).

The Torah reports that "*she* spied the basket among the reeds." Were there not also maidservants present? Perhaps the Torah should have said that *they* spied the basket. One midrash concludes that of course everyone physically saw the basket. However, the Torah distinguishes between the mindset of Pharaoh's daughter and that of her maidservants. When Pharaoh's daughter wanted to save Moses, her maidservants critically reminded her that her own father had made the decree (*Sotah* 12b)!

A third example: the Torah notes that Pharaoh's daughter "made him her son." Why add this seemingly superfluous phrase? One midrash concludes that Pharaoh's daughter hugged and kissed Moses as though he really was her own child (*Exodus Rabbah* 1:31).

The aforementioned questions and responses are not likely to be raised by *pashtanim*, but they still have bearing on the textual account of Pharaoh's daughter. There is something remarkable about the courage of Pharaoh's daughter, who defied her own father and society. In addition, several midrashim assume that Pharaoh's daughter must have learned Hebrew in order to name Moses using a Hebrew etymology. Midrashically, this combination points to some form of "conversion" from the paganism and immorality of her father, associates, and entire society.

On a different plane, the Torah reports that a grown Moses left the palace endowed with an incredible moral sense. In short order he killed an Egyptian taskmaster, intervened in an Israelite quarrel, and stepped into a struggle among Midianites at the well. Where did this moral fortitude come from? Seemingly, it derived at least partially from

Pharaoh's daughter. Moses' defiance of Pharaoh and society parallels the heroism of his adoptive mother. Moses also instantly identified with his brethren, the Israelites. Perhaps Pharaoh's daughter, who could have raised him as an Egyptian, reminded him who he really was.[9]

Since Moses left the palace as a young adult, Pharaoh's daughter forever lost her beloved adopted son whom she had raised as her own. She likely was heartbroken, but also incredibly proud. She had raised a child who shared her vision of looking beyond the pagan immorality that characterized Egyptian society.

From the Torah itself we will never know who Pharaoh's daughter was or even her name. But her moral courage in rescuing Moses against her father's orders and in the presence of her maidservants, and her nurturing Moses' moral and Israelite identity, changed the world by her rescuing and then raising the greatest individual who ever lived. We may view Pharaoh's daughter's break from Egyptian immorality as a form of conversion from all Egyptian society from Pharaoh down to the maidservants.

Turning to Chronicles, we find a named daughter of Pharaoh in the Judahite genealogy: "These were the sons of Bithiah daughter of Pharaoh, whom Mered married" (I Chronicles 4:18).[10] Midrashically, this woman is identified with Moses' rescuer. The name Bithiah is understood as "bat Ya-h," or "the daughter of God." One midrash remarks, "God told Pharaoh's daughter: Moses was not your child, yet you treated him as you would your own son. Even though you are not My daughter, I will call you My daughter" (Leviticus Rabbah 1:3).

People often act heroically though they might be forgotten from conscious memory. However, their impact can transform individuals and change the world. The silent yet powerful impact of Hur and Pharaoh's daughter in the Torah, fleshed out by various midrashic traditions, represents this type of greatness.

NOTES

1. See Hayyim Angel, "The Paradox of *Parshanut*: Are Our Eyes on the Text, or on the Commentators, Review Essay of *Pirkei Nehama: Nehama Leibowitz Memorial Volume*," *Tradition* 38:4 (Winter 2004), pp. 112–128; reprinted in Angel, *Peshat Isn't So Simple: Essays on Developing a Religious Methodology to Bible Study* (New York: Kodesh Press, 2014), pp. 36–57; *Conversations* 21 (Winter 2015), pp. 127–144.

2. Surveys of traditional understandings of the term *peshat* can be found in Rabbi Menahem M. Kasher, *Torah Shelemah*, 17 (1956), pp. 286–312; David Weiss-Halivni, *Peshat and Derash: Plain and Applied Meaning in Rabbinic Exegesis* (Oxford: Oxford University Press, 1991), pp. 52–88; Moshe Ahrend, "Towards a Definition of the Term '*Peshuto Shel Mikra*'" (Hebrew), in *HaMikra BeRe'i Mefarshav: Sara Kamin Memorial Volume*, ed. Sara Japhet (Jerusalem: The Magnes Press, 1994), pp. 237–261.

3. While later rabbinic commentators generally defer to the halakhic rulings of the Talmud, that principle is not universally adopted. See, e.g., Marc B. Shapiro, "Maimonidean Halakhah and Superstition," in *Studies in Maimonides and His Interpreters* (Scranton: University of Scranton Press, 2008), pp. 95–150. Shapiro documents many examples where Rambam deviated from talmudic halakhic rulings (or simply ignored them) when he believed them to be based on superstitions. Given the reservations post-talmudic commentators generally have in disregarding talmudic rulings, Shapiro concludes that Rambam was "unprecedented and courageous" in taking those positions. His conclusion highlights how unusual Rambam's stance was among halakhic decisors. While fascinating and important in its own right, this topic takes us well beyond our point of discussion.

4. See, e.g., Rabbi Marc D. Angel, "Authority and Dissent: A Discussion of Boundaries," *Tradition* 25:2 (Winter 1990), pp. 18–27; Rabbi Haim David Halevi, *Aseh Lekha Rav*, vol. 5, resp. 49 (pp. 304–307); Rabbi Michael Rosensweig, "*Elu va-Elu Divre Elokim Hayyim*: Halakhic Pluralism and Theories of Controversy," *Tradition* 26:3 (Spring 1992), pp. 4–23; Marc Saperstein, *Decoding the Rabbis: A Thirteenth-Century Commentary on the Aggadah* (Cambridge MA: Harvard University Press, 1980), pp. 1–20;

Rabbi Moshe Shamah, "On Interpreting Midrash," in *Where the Yeshiva Meets the University: Traditional and Academic Approaches to Tanakh Study*, ed. Hayyim Angel, *Conversations* 15 (Winter 2013), pp. 27–39.

5.   Translation from the Maimonides Heritage Center, https://www.mhcny. org/qt/1005.pdf. Accessed March 15, 2016.

6.   See further in Rabbi Marc Angel, "Reflections on Torah Education and Mis-Education," *Conversations* 24 (Winter 2016), pp. 18–32; Rabbi Amnon Bazak, *Ad HaYom HaZeh: Until This Day: Fundamental Questions in Bible Teaching* (Hebrew), ed. Yoshi Farajun (Tel Aviv: Yediot Aharonot, 2013), pp. 349–431; Rabbi Nahum E. Rabinovitch, "Faith in the Sages: What Is It?" (Hebrew), in *Mesillot Bilvavam* (Ma'alei Adumim: Ma'aliyot, 2014), pp. 103–114.

7.   *Tanhuma Tetzavveh* 10 spells out the textual derivation from Hur's mention in Exodus 24:14 and subsequent absence in the Golden Calf narrative. Cf. *Sanhedrin* 7a.

8.   This midrash assumes that God commanded the building of the Tabernacle after the Golden Calf episode, rather than simultaneous to it.

9.   Cf. Rabbi Elhanan Samet, *Iyyunim BeParashot HaShavua*, second series, vol. 1 (Hebrew) ed. Ayal Fishler (Ma'aleh Adumim: Ma'aliyot Press, 2004), pp. 244-245. Offering an alternative possibility, Joseph H. Hertz surmises that Moses' formative years nursing with his mother enabled Jochebed to teach Moses about his Israelite identity (*The Pentateuch and Haftorahs*, [London: Soncino Press, 1968], p. 210).

10. Cf. *Megillah* 13a: "These are the sons of Bithiah whom Mered took" (I Chronicles 4:18): Was Mered his name? Was not Caleb his name? The Holy One, blessed be He, said: Let Caleb who rebelled [*marad*] against the plan of the spies come and take the daughter of Pharaoh who rebelled against the idols of her father's house." In this midrashic identification, Moses and Hur would now be half-stepbrothers.

Traditional and Academic Tanakh Study

Opportunities and Challenges*

Tanakh lies at the heart and soul of Judaism. The Talmud and Midrash, Jewish philosophy and mysticism, and Jewish thought all find their deepest roots in the Bible. For millennia, Jews and other faith communities have been transformed by this unparalleled collection of 24 books. Tanakh is accessible and enjoyable to small children and to the most sophisticated scholars and thinkers. It is a singular privilege to encounter its sacred words, to engage with its eternal messages, and to be galvanized to greater ethical and social action and spiritual growth as a result of our study.[1]

From the perspective of contemporary religious students of Tanakh, we have remarkable opportunities today. Scholars publish critical editions of our classical commentators so that we have access to the most accurate texts from our greatest teachers. They discover and publish previously obscure rabbinic works, enabling us to broaden our understanding of the range of interpretation in the classical period. They also advance the field of biblical study in areas including, but not limited to, literary analysis, archaeology and history, and linguistics. The information readily available in books, online resources, and classes is breathtaking.

---

* This essay appeared originally in *Conversations* 27 (Winter 2017), pp. 130-136.

At the same time, however, these opportunities pose serious challenges to our enterprise. How do we balance this flood of knowledge and methodology with the fact that many scholars in the field are not Orthodox Jews and therefore bring their own assumptions and biases to their work? Are there means for sorting through which information and methodology is beneficial for our religious growth and which must be discarded or modified? Ultimately, the litmus test of success for our study of Tanakh is that it deepens our religious commitments and inspires us to greater ethical behavior. How do we shape the contours of this discussion to maximize those benefits and characterize that process with intellectual honesty and integrity?

When we learn and teach Tanakh properly, we convey a sense of holiness and reverence, coupled with respect for individuality and intellectual struggle with our most sacred texts and traditions. Tanakh has the singular ability to inspire and edify people of all ages and backgrounds. The potent combination of rabbinic commentary and contemporary scholarship enables our minds, hearts, and souls to complement one another in a holistic spiritual and intellectual experience. The maturation of sophisticated Tanakh study provides us with a system with which to navigate the complicated contours of scholarship and religious growth. Rabbis and educators have the immense responsibility to sort through available information, commentaries, and methodologies in order to steer the discussion for the benefit of the community.

In theory, the text analysis in the yeshiva and the academy could be identical, since both engage in the quest for truth. The fundamental difference between the two is that in the yeshiva, we study Tanakh as a means to understanding revelation as the expression of God's will. The scholarly conclusions we reach impact directly on our lives and our religious worldview. In the academy, on the other hand, truth is pursued as an intellectual activity for its own sake, usually as an end in itself. There also are no accompanying beliefs in the revelation of the text.

The ostensible conflicts between traditional and academic scholarship have led some scholars, including several who iden-tify with the Orthodox community, to conclude that traditional faith is incompatible with scholarship. This supposition has led some to reject traditional belief outright, or to radically redefine faith to make it compatible with their scholarly conclusions, or to radically reinterpret classical sources in an attempt to justify such paradigm shifts as being within tradition. These positions have led to counter-reactions in some Orthodox circles that adopt excessively dogmatic and restrictive positions to prohibit scholarly inquiry or *peshat* learning altogether. Both sides may be motivated by a pro-found and authentic religious desire to connect to God and the Torah, but they distort aspects of tradition and create dangerous and unnecessary rifts between us.

In *Ad ha-Yom ha-Zeh*, Rabbi Amnon Bazak, one of the bright stars at Yeshivat Har Etzion and its affiliated Herzog College, offers a sophisticated understanding of Tanakh and our faith axioms while simultaneously being fully open to contemporary scholarship. Addressing the fact that many in the Orthodox world disregard contemporary academic scholarship, Rabbi Bazak offers three rea-sons why such willful ignorance is inexcusable: (1) On educational grounds these issues are widely publicized, and therefore rabbis and religious educators must be able to address them intelligently. (2) Many of the questions are genuine, and must be taken seriously on scholarly grounds. (3) We often gain a better understanding of Tanakh with the aid of contemporary scholarship.

Rabbi Bazak's central premise is that we must distinguish between facts and compelling tools of analysis, which must be considered in our learning; and the assumptions of scholars, which we reject when they conflict with traditional beliefs. Rabbi Bazak argues that nothing based on facts forces one to choose between faith and scholarship.[2]

The growing popularity of what Rabbi Shalom Carmy calls the "literary-theological" approach to Tanakh study has been transforming the way we approach our most sacred texts. This methodology demands a finely tuned reading of the text, along with a focus on the religious significance of the passage. The premises of this approach include: (1) Oral Law and classical commentaries are central to the way we understand the revealed word of God, and (2) it is vital to study biblical passages in their literary and historical context.[3]

Over the past two centuries, analysis of literary tools, comparative linguistics, and the discovery of a wealth of ancient texts and artifacts have contributed immensely to our understanding the rich tapestry and complexity of biblical texts. Much also has improved since the 1970's as a result of the literary revolution in biblical scholarship. After generations of dissecting the Torah and the rest of Tanakh, many Bible scholars have recognized that the Torah and later biblical books can be analyzed effectively as unified texts. Every word is valuable. Passages are multilayered. Understanding the interplay between texts is vital.

Great traditional scholars of the previous generation such as the authors and editors of the *Da'at Mikra* commentary series,[4] Professor Nehama Leibowitz,[5] and Rabbi Mordechai Breuer,[6] exemplified different aspects of how one could benefit from the information and methodology of academic Bible scholarship through the prism of traditional faith. Similarly, the prolific writings of leading contemporary rabbinic scholars such as Yoel Bin-Nun,[7] Elhanan Samet,[8] and Shalom Carmy[9] are intellectually and spiritually stimulating, as they benefit from the academy while working from the viewpoint of the yeshiva.[10]

The ideal learning framework espouses traditional beliefs and studies as a means to a religious end while striving for intellectual openness and honesty. Reaching this synthesis is difficult, since it requires passionate commitment alongside an effort to be detached while learning in order to refine knowledge and understanding.

To benefit from contemporary biblical scholarship properly, we first must understand our own tradition—to have a grasp of our texts, assumptions, and the range of traditional interpretations. This educational process points to a much larger issue. For example, studying comparative religion should be broadening. However, people unfamiliar with their own tradition, or who know it primarily from non-traditional teachers or textbooks, will have little more than a shallow basis for comparison.

Religious scholarship benefits from contemporary findings—both information and methodology. Outside perspectives prod us to be more critical in our own learning. On the other side of the equation, the academy stands to benefit from those who are heirs to thousands of years of tradition, who approach every word of Tanakh with awe and reverence, and who care deeply about the intricate relationship between texts.[11] The academy also must become more aware of its own underlying biases.

Ultimately, we must recognize the strengths and weaknesses in the approaches of the yeshivah and the academy. By doing so, we can study the eternal words of Tanakh using the best of classical and contemporary scholarship. This process gives us an ever-refining ability to deepen our relationship with God, the world community, and ourselves. It also enables us to build bridges within our community.

Dr. Norman Lamm has set the tone for this inquiry:

> Torah is a "Torah of truth," and to hide from the facts is to distort that truth into myth.… It is this kind of position which honest men, particularly honest believers in God and Torah, must adopt at all times, and especially in our times. Conventional dogmas, even if endowed with the authority of an Aristotle—ancient or modern—must be tested vigorously. If they are found wanting, we need not bother with them. But if they are found to be substantially correct, we may not overlook them. We must then use newly discovered truths the better to understand our Torah—the "Torah of truth."[12]

The eternally relevant vision of the Torah and prophets is available for the taking. What we make of the journey is up to us, to learn and transform, and work on building the ideal self and society envisioned by our prophetic tradition as we develop our own relationships between God and humanity through the inspired words of Tanakh.

Our early morning daily liturgy challenges us: "Ever shall a person be God-fearing in secret as in public, with truth in his heart as on his lips." May we be worthy of pursuing that noble combination.

NOTES

1. Some of this article is adapted from Hayyim Angel, Editor's Introduction in *Where the Yeshiva Meets the University: Traditional and Academic Approaches to Tanakh Study*, ed. Hayyim Angel. *Conversations* 15 (Winter 2013), pp. v–vii; Hayyim Angel, "The Yeshivah and the Academy: How We Can Learn from One Another in Biblical Scholarship," in Angel, *Peshat Isn't So Simple: Essays on Developing a Religious Methodology to Bible Study* (New York: Kodesh Press, 2014), pp. 28–35.

2. Rabbi Amnon Bazak, *Ad ha-Yom ha-Zeh: Until This Day: Fundamental Questions in Bible Teaching* (Hebrew), ed. Yoshi Farajun (Tel Aviv: Yediot Aharonot, 2013). See also review essay of Hayyim Angel, "Faith and Scholarship Can Walk Together: Rabbi Amnon Bazak on the Challenges of Academic Bible Study in Traditional Learning," *Tradition* 47:3 (Fall 2014), pp. 78–88.

3. Rabbi Shalom Carmy, "A Room with a View, but a Room of Our Own," in *Modern Scholarship in the Study of Torah: Contributions and Limitations*, ed. Shalom Carmy (Northvale, NJ: Jason Aronson Inc., 1996), pp. 1–38.

4. After completing the series, two of its leading contributors and editors, Yehudah Kiel and Amos Hakham, wrote a short book describing the history and goals of the series, *Epilogue to the Da'at Mikra Commentary* (Hebrew) (Jerusalem: Keter, 2003).

5. For more on her work, see especially Yael Unterman, *Nehama Leibowitz: Teacher and Bible Scholar* (Jerusalem: Urim, 2009); *Pirkei Nehama: Nehama Leibowitz Memorial Volume* (Hebrew), ed. Moshe Ahrend, Ruth Ben-Meir, and Gavriel H. Cohn (Jerusalem: Eliner Library, The Joint Authority for Jewish Zionist Education, Department for Torah and Culture in the Diaspora, 2001); Hayyim Angel, Review Essay: *"Pirkei Nehama: Nehama Leibowitz Memorial Volume*: The Paradox of *Parshanut*: Are Our Eyes on the Text, or on the Commentators?" in Angel, *Peshat Isn't So Simple: Essays on Developing a Religious Methodology to Bible Study* (New York: Kodesh Press, 2014), pp. 36–57.

6. For analysis of Rabbi Breuer's method, see Rabbi Amnon Bazak, *Ad ha-Yom ha-Zeh*, pp. 109–139; Rabbi Shalom Carmy, "Concepts of

Scripture in Mordechai Breuer," in *Jewish Concepts of Scripture: A Comparative Introduction*, ed. Benjamin D. Sommer (New York: New York University Press, 2012), pp. 267–279; Rabbi Meir Ekstein, "Rabbi Mordechai Breuer and Modern Orthodox Biblical Commentary," *Tradition* 33:3 (Spring 1999), pp. 6–23. For a collection of Rabbi Breuer's articles on his methodology, and important responses to his work, see *The Theory of Aspects of Rabbi Mordechai Breuer* (Hebrew), ed. Yosef Ofer (Alon Shevut: Tevunot, 2005). For case studies of Rabbi Breuer's methodology, see especially Rabbi Breuer's *Pirkei Mo'adot* (Jerusalem: Horev, 1989), *Pirkei Bereshit* (Alon Shevut: Tevunot, 1998), and *Pirkei Mikra'ot* (Alon Shevut: Tevunot, 2009).

7. For an overview of Rabbi Bin-Nun's methodology, including citations to many of his published articles through 2006, see Hayyim Angel, "*Torat Hashem Temima:* The Contributions of Rav Yoel Bin-Nun to Religious Tanakh Study," in Angel, *The Keys to the Palace: Essays Exploring the Religious Value of Reading the Bible* (New York: Kodesh Press, 2017), pp. 36-57.

8. *Iyyunim be-Parashot ha-Shavua* (series 1, 2, and 3), ed. Ayal Fishler (Ma'aleh Adumim: Ma'aliyot, 2002, 2004, 2012). For an overview of Rabbi Samet's methodology, see Hayyim Angel, "Review of Rabbi Elhanan Samet, *Iyyunim be-Parashot ha-Shavua,*" in Angel, *Through an Opaque Lens*, revised second edition (New York: Kodesh Press, 2013), pp. 6–18. See also Rabbi Samet's books, *Pirkei Eliyahu* (Ma'aleh Adumim: Ma'aliyot, 2003), *Pirkei Elisha* (Ma'aleh Adumim: Ma'aliyot, 2007), *Iyyunim BeMizmorei Tehillim* (Tel Aviv: Yediot Aharonot, 2012). Many of his articles are archived in English translation at the Virtual Beit Midrash of Yeshivat Har Etzion, at http://www.vbm-torah.org.

9. Rabbi Carmy gives an overview of his own methodology in "A Room with a View, but a Room of Our Own," in *Modern Scholarship in the Study of Torah: Contributions and Limitations*, ed. Shalom Carmy (Northvale, NJ: Jason Aronson, 1996), pp. 1–38. See also especially his "To Get the Better of Words: An Apology for *Yir'at Shamayim* in Academic Jewish Studies," *Torah U-Madda Journal* 2 (1990), pp. 7–24; "Always Connect," in *Where the Yeshiva Meets the University: Traditional and*

Academic Approaches to Tanakh Study, ed. Hayyim Angel, *Conversations* 15 (Winter 2013), pp. 1–12. For a bibliography of his published writings through 2012, see *Rav Shalom Banayikh: Essays Presented to Rabbi Shalom Carmy by Friends and Students in Celebration of Forty Years of Teaching*, ed. Hayyim Angel and Yitzchak Blau (Jersey City, NJ: Ktav, 2012), pp. 403–414.

10. For further discussion and references, see Hayyim Angel, "The Literary-Theological Study of Tanakh," afterword to Moshe Sokolow, *Tanakh: An Owner's Manual: Authorship, Canonization, Masoretic Text, Exegesis, Modern Scholarship and Pedagogy* (Brooklyn, NY: Ktav, 2015), pp. 192–207.

11. Cf. William H. C. Propp: "Generations of Bible students are taught that the goal of criticism is to find contradiction as a first not a last resort, and to attribute every verse, nay every word, to an author or editor. That is what we do for a living. But the folly of harmonizing away every contradiction, every duplication, is less than the folly of chopping the text into dozens of particles or redactional levels. After all, the *harmonizing* reader may at least recreate the editors' understanding of their product. But the *atomizing* reader posits and analyzes literary materials whose existence is highly questionable" (*Exodus 19-40* Anchor Bible [New York: Doubleday, 2006], p. 734). At the conclusion of his commentary, Propp explains that he often consulted medieval rabbinic commentators precisely because they saw unity in the composite whole of the Torah (p. 808). See also Michael V. Fox: "Medieval Jewish commentary has largely been neglected in academic Bible scholarship, though a great many of the ideas of modern commentators arose first among the medievals, and many of their brightest insights are absent from later exegesis" (*Proverbs 1-9* Anchor Bible [New York: Doubleday, 2000], p. 12).

12. Rabbi Norman Lamm, *Faith and Doubt: Studies in Traditional Jewish Thought* (New York: Ktav, 1971), pp. 124–125.

DOGMA, HERESY, AND CLASSICAL DEBATES

CREATING JEWISH UNITY IN AN AGE OF CONFUSION*

INTRODUCTION

Judaism is built upon the basic tenets of belief in one God, divine revelation of the Torah including an Oral Law, divine providence, reward and punishment, and a messianic redemption. Although there have been debates over the precise definitions and boundaries of these principles, they have been universally accepted as part of our tradition.[1]

The question for believing Jews today is: how should we relate to the overwhelming majority of contemporary Jews, who likely do not fully believe in classical Jewish beliefs? Two medieval models shed light on this question.

RAMBAM: DOGMATIC APPROACH

Rambam insists that proper belief is essential. Whether one intentionally rejects Jewish beliefs, or is simply mistaken or uninformed, non-belief leads to one's exclusion from the Jewish community and from the World to Come:

---

* This essay appeared originally in *Conversations* 27 (Winter 2017), pp. 22-29.

When a person affirms all these Principles, and clarifies his faith in them, he becomes part of the Jewish People. It is a mitzvah to love him, have mercy on him, and show him all the love and brotherhood that God has instructed us to show our fellow Jews. Even if he has transgressed out of desire and the overpowering influence of his base nature, he will be punished accordingly but he will have a share in the World to Come. But one who denies any of these Principles has excluded himself from the Jewish People and denied the essence [of Judaism]. He is called a heretic, an *epikoros*, and "one who has cut off the seedlings." It is a mitzvah to hate and destroy such a person, as it says (Psalms 139:21), "Those who hate You, God, I shall hate" (Rambam, *Introduction to Perek Helek*).

Scholars of Rambam generally explain that Rambam did not think of afterlife as a reward. Rather, it is a natural consequence of one's religious-intellectual development. Only one prepared for afterlife may gain acceptance. Although Rambam did not invent Jewish beliefs, he did innovate this position of Judaism being primarily a community of believers in a set of dogmas.[2]

Professor Menachem Kellner explains that prior to Rambam, Jewish faith was defined by an experiential relationship with God and the Torah. There were of course underlying beliefs in God, the revelation of the Torah, the Oral Law, God's personal involvement and providence, and the Messiah; but these beliefs were not commanded, nor were they too precisely defined. Kellner suggests that Rambam's innovative view arose from the surrounding Muslim culture. During that period, Muslims asked, (a) who is a Muslim and who is an unbeliever? (b) Who will achieve salvation and who is damned? To be a Muslim in good standing and achieve salvation requires one to have proper beliefs, regardless of one's actions. Therefore, the need to define proper belief was a central concern in Rambam's world.[3] Judaism also needed to distinguish itself from Islam since both are monotheistic faiths, and Jews faced intense pressure to convert to Islam in order to attain better social status.[4]

Rambam's attempt to define the tenets of Jewish faith follows in the footsteps of the Mishnah in *Sanhedrin* 90a, which is the only place in the Talmud where beliefs are presented in dogmatic form:

> All Israel have a portion in the World to Come, for it is written, "Your people are all righteous; they shall inherit the land forever, the branch of My planting, the work of My hands, that I be glorified." But the following have no portion therein: He who maintains that resurrection is not a biblical doctrine, the Torah was not divinely revealed, and an *epikoros*....

Clearly, this Mishnah is not a roster of all Jewish belief, but rather focuses on the issues that fractured the Jewish community at that time. The Sages stressed these particular tenets of faith in order to distinguish the faithful rabbinic community from Sadducees and other sectarian groups.[5]

Although these efforts by the Mishnah are significant in terms of expressing proper Jewish belief, Rambam goes much further than the Mishnah by defining Jews as a communion of true believers. This innovative position opened the door to heretical exclusions even when one was not trying to exclude himself or herself from the Jewish community.[6]

RA'AVAD-DURAN-ALBO: MISTAKEN, NOT HERETICS

Rambam (*Hilkhot Teshuvah* 3:7) rules that there are several categories of heretics. One of those is the person who believes that God has physical attributes. Yet, Ra'avad (Rabbi Abraham b. David, 1125–1198) disagrees, since even some great rabbis mistakenly concluded that God does have physical attributes:[7]

> Why did [Rambam] call such a person a heretic? Several greater and better rabbis than he thought [that God does have a body and likeness] based on what they see in biblical verses and even more so from rabbinic teachings that can confuse the thoughts.

Ra'avad agrees with Rambam that God is incorporeal. However, he insists that it is incorrect to label as heretics those who mistakenly believe otherwise. They are believing Jews who made an honest error based on an overly literal reading of Tanakh and Midrash.

Following Ra'avad's approach, Rabbi Shimon b. Tzemah Duran and Rabbi Yosef Albo maintained that one is considered a heretic only if one willfully denies a principle of faith or willfully affirms a principle denied by the Torah.[8] Duran even cites statements by Rambam that Duran considers to be beyond the pale of Jewish belief. He concludes that Rambam is not a heretic for holding these views, but reached mistaken views out of purity of motive. It should be stressed that Duran agrees that there *are* standard beliefs, and rabbis should correct the errors of those Jews who have mistaken beliefs. However, this does not mean excluding them from the community as heretics, but embracing and teaching them.

In his extensive survey of medieval thinkers, Professor Menachem Kellner concludes that the decisive majority support this latter view, rather than the exclusionary dogmatic position of Rambam.[9]

Halakhah defines Jewishness by birth and nationhood, and not by belief. We ideally want all Jews to learn, observe, and believe in the Torah and tradition. However, we should not exclude as heretics those who fall short unless they intentionally wish to exclude themselves from the community.[10] Jews who make honest mistakes or who are ignorant of proper Jewish belief are not to be labeled as heretics. Rather, we should do what we can to educate them.

It is important to note that Rambam himself differentiated between the original Karaites, who were true heretics who broke from the Jewish community, and their followers and descendants who did not know better because they grew up as Karaites (*Hilkhot Mamrim* 3:3). After stating that one who denies the Oral Law is a heretic (*Hilkhot Mamrim* 3:1–2), Rambam exonerates the Karaites of his day for having been raised with erroneous beliefs. Menachem Kellner explains that in Rambam's system of thought, there was no latitude for someone who makes an innocent error regarding Rambam's first five principles of faith that pertain to the essence of God. In that arena, if a Jew believes that God has a body, that person is a heretic. However, the Karaite error is within Rambam's eighth principle, as they deny the revelation of an Oral Law revealed to Moses along with the Written Torah. In this respect, the original Karaites who actively denied this principle of faith are heretics, but later generations who grew up with this miseducation should be deemed as ignorant against their will, rather than as heretics.[11]

CONCLUSION

Moving this discussion to a contemporary communal level, Menachem Kellner contends that Orthodox society must properly frame the question in terms of its relationship with non-Orthodox society. If we ask how much heresy we should tolerate, we already have lost the battle. Pluralism, in the sense of saying that non-Orthodox and non-halakhic ideologies are legitimate within Torah and *halakhah*, is an impossible position for an Orthodox Jew to hold. Declaring that most non-Orthodox Jews are in the category of *tinok she-nishbah*—one who was kidnapped and raised among heathens and therefore no longer accountable for one's religious behavior—may promote greater tolerance, but is insulting.

Kellner concludes that one should ask instead: What can we do to enhance the future of the Jewish people? A healthy family can survive disputes. We should not ignore the disputes; but areas of agreement, our shared past, and a shared concern for our future as a people, should bring us together despite fundamental differences in belief and observance.[12]

We may define the question differently. If we view ourselves as a community of believers inside a box, and everyone else as outside that box, then Rambam gives us an objective standard of who is in our group and who is excluded. If, however, we define ourselves more positively as believing Jews who embrace God, Torah, and all Jews, then we would espouse the view of Ra'avad-Duran-Albo, who maintain proper belief while considering those who reject or do not know these beliefs as mistaken or ignorant rather than as heretics.

The halakhic definition of a Jew is one who has Jewish mother or who is a halakhic convert. Not every Jew lives a full Jewish life, but there is a continuum with more and less committed Jews, rather than insiders and outsiders. The approach espoused by Ra'avad-Duran-Albo, which appears closer to the original concept of Jewish belief, also represents a more productive means of addressing today's fragmented society from within tradition. We stand for an eternal set of beliefs and practices, and we embrace and teach all Jews as we build our community together.[13]

No less significantly, it is critical for believing Jews to understand that there are many legitimate paths within Jewish tradition. Many rifts are created when rabbis and others insist that their path is the only true path, while others are considered wrong or not even acknowledged. One of the great nineteenth-century rabbis, Rabbi Naftali Tzvi Yehudah Berlin (Netziv), expressed his fear based on the realities of his time that faithful Jews may brand other faithful Jews as heretics for following other legitimate paths within tradition:

> It is not difficult to imagine reaching this situation in our time, Heaven forbid, that if one of the faithful thinks that a certain person does not follow his way in the service of God, then he will judge him as a heretic... the people of God will be destroyed, Heaven forfend (Meshiv Davar, I:44).

THE INCLUSIVE COMMUNAL MODEL

One of the beacons of light emanating from the Sephardic world, and from many Ashkenazic communities in the modern age is its inclusive communal model. Rather than creating separate synagogues for the devoutly Orthodox, or splintering into movements or denominations that fracture the Jewish community, this model calls for synagogues to be faithful to Jewish tradition and to welcome Jews from the entire spectrum of religious observance.

In the nineteenth and twentieth centuries, Jews of Germany, America, and several other major communities splintered into denominations and movements. They led us to today's painful fragmentation with no easy resolutions presenting themselves going forward. The inclusive communal model provides a desperately needed alternative to the realities of today.[14]

So why did so much of the Jewish world miss this point? In addition to the historical circumstances, there is a good conceptual answer to that question, explored by Rabbi Jonathan Sacks in his book, *Community of Faith*.[15] Rabbi Sacks observes that there is a great challenge in the inclusive model: It is the least consistent, and we greatly value consistency. Some people asked: Why belong to a traditional synagogue that preaches ideals so different from my lifestyle? Why not build synagogue communities that espouse messages more consistent with my values?

Others criticized the institutions and their rabbis. How can an Orthodox synagogue be a welcoming home to people who do not live by Orthodox standards? We should build separate synagogues and schools exclusively for those who are entirely faithful to tradition. This desire for greater consistency contributed to the fracturing of the Jewish community.

These are genuine challenges to the inclusive communal model. Our response to these challenges is the positive agenda of a unified faith community. Those who join it do not necessarily adhere to all of the *mitzvot* or Jewish beliefs in the traditional sense. However, they want to belong to a congregation that in its public and collective expressions remains loyal to the principles by which Jews have always lived. As a result of this model, Jews who personally do not observe many *mitzvot* can develop a profound respect for their synagogue and community, because they correctly understand that it faithfully represents Jewish tradition.

Rabbis and communal leadership also need to be open to all Jews, and work to create a welcoming environment where that attitude is fostered throughout the community. Our challenge is to the build an ideal communal setting, faithful to tradition, and welcoming to all Jews. We need to set the standard by which all participants are encouraged to bridge the gaps between their lives and the ideals of the Torah. This vision may be easier said than done in today's climate, but it is critical to advance it as a productive alternative to the unfortunate reality we currently experience.

Judaism is both a peoplehood and a religious covenant. Ideally, all Jews should be committed to both dimensions of the Torah. In an age when many Jews have lost or diminished their religious connection, however, our commitment to peoplehood must prevail to include Jews who are not fully committed to the Torah or Jewish belief. The winners will be the Torah and the Jewish people.

NOTES

1. See Marc B. Shapiro, *The Limits of Orthodox Theology: Maimonides' Thirteen Principles Reappraised* (Oxford: Littman Library of Jewish Civilization, 2004); Rabbi Yitzchak Blau, "Flexibility with a Firm Foundation: On Maintaining Jewish Dogma," *Torah U-Madda Journal* 12 (2004), pp. 179–191.

2. See Menachem Kellner, *Dogma in Medieval Jewish Thought: From Maimonides to Abravanel* (Oxford: Littman Library of Jewish Civilization, 1986); Menachem Kellner, *Must a Jew Believe Anything?* (London: Littman Library of Jewish Civilization, 1999); David Berger, *Tradition* 33:4 (Summer 1999), pp. 81–89; Menachem Kellner's second edition of *Must a Jew Believe Anything?* (2006) contains a response to David Berger's review. See also Seth (Avi) Kadish ("Jewish Dogma after Maimonides: Semantics or Substance?" *Hebrew Union College Annual* 86 [2015], pp. 195–263), who discusses the need to understand Rambam's dogmas in the broader context of medieval rabbinic thought. According to Kadish, the medieval authorities debated primarily the very nature of God and the Torah, and not the technicalities of dogma. The consensus resulting from that debate was to reject Rambam's dogmatic conception of the Torah.

3. Kellner, *Dogma in Medieval Jewish Thought*, pp. 7–9.

4. Kellner, *Must a Jew Believe Anything?*, pp. 49–50.

5. Rabbi Jonathan Sacks observes that instead of writing treatises or systematic lists of beliefs, the Sages included central Jewish beliefs in the prayer liturgy. The emphasis in the second blessing of the Amidah on the future resurrection of the dead, for example, ensured that sectarians who denied the resurrection would be unable to lead the prayer service, and would be discouraged from attending synagogue altogether ("The *Siddur*: Book of Jewish Faith," in *Mi-Tokh Ha-Ohel: The Weekday Prayers*, ed. Daniel Z. Feldman and Stuart W. Halpern [New Milford, CT: Maggid, 2014], pp. xiii–xxi).

6. Menachem Kellner, *Must a Jew Believe Anything?*, p. 2.

7. For a survey of rabbinic positions on God's incorporeality, see Marc B. Shapiro, *The Limits of Orthodox Theology*, pp. 45–70.

8. Kellner, *Dogma in Medieval Jewish Thought*, pp. 99–107.

9. Kellner, *Must a Jew Believe Anything?*, p. 68. Aside from Rambam, only Rabbis Abraham Bibago and Yitzhak Abarbanel disallowed error in belief and considered people making those errors heretics.

10. Kellner, *Must a Jew Believe Anything?*, pp. 111–126.

11. *Ibid.*, pp. 84–85.

12. *Ibid.*, pp. 98–99, 111–126.

13. See also Rabbi Dov Linzer, "The Discourse of Halakhic Inclusiveness," *Conversations* 1 (Spring 2008), pp. 1–5; Menachem Kellner, "Must We Have Heretics?" *Conversations* 1 (Spring 2008), pp. 6–10.

14. See further discussion in Rabbi Marc D. Angel, "Other Thoughts about Jewish Pluralism," in Angel, *Seeking Good, Speaking Peace: Collected Essays of Rabbi Marc D. Angel*, ed. Hayyim Angel (Hoboken, NJ: Ktav, 1994), pp. 24–35.

15. Rabbi Jonathan Sacks, *Community of Faith* (London: Peter Halban, 1995).

BATTLING FOR THE
SOUL OF ORTHODOXY

THE ESSENTIAL TEACHINGS OF
RABBI MARC D. ANGEL[*]

Rabbi Marc D. Angel has been one of the most prolific rabbinic scholars during the past 50 years. He has written or edited 37 books, and hundreds of scholarly articles and shorter pieces in various media. He served a distinguished career as Rabbi of Congregation Shearith Israel in New York City, and since 2007 as the Founder and Director of the Institute for Jewish Ideas and Ideals. He has served in many communal and rabbinic leadership capacities, as well.

The task of writing an article to encapsulate the extensive work of Rabbi Angel is reminiscent of the celebrated talmudic story of the prospective convert who demanded of Hillel to teach him the entire Torah while the prospective convert stood on one foot. Hillel responded: "What is hateful to you, do not to your neighbor: that is the whole Torah, while the rest is the commentary thereof; go and learn it" (*Shabbat* 31a). My goal in this essay is to present "on one foot" Rabbi Angel's central ideas and ideals which he has promoted over the course of 50 years.

---

[*] This essay appeared as a foreword to a collection of my father's essays, published as *Conversations* 34 (Autumn 2019), in honor of his serving for fifty years in the rabbinate.

◇◇◇

Rabbi Angel believes that one must first establish the proper intellectual foundations for an ideal vision of Judaism, and then attempt to build a great personal religious life and Torah community from the ground up. Judaism begins with a profound and abiding belief in God, that God revealed the Torah to the people of Israel through Moses as an eternal covenant, and that there is an accompanying Oral Law to the Written Torah. Judaism also maintains that the rabbinic sages throughout the generations have had the authority to interpret texts and traditions to apply the eternal principles of *halakhah* to an ever-changing world.

What today is known as Orthodoxy is the faithful reflection of Jewish tradition. Streams of Judaism that are not committed to divine revelation or to *halakhah* cannot be authentic representations of classic Jewish thought.

Living a proper halakhic life creates a deep, intimate relationship with God. Interiority, humility, love of humanity and a desire to improve society are proper manifestations of a righteous life. Authentic religion is not about showiness, disdain for others, or authoritarianism.

The aforementioned arguments are easy to establish from within traditional Jewish sources, and Rabbi Angel therefore devotes relatively little energy to defend them. The lion's share of his work is dedicated to a different theme, namely, delineating and advocating for what he considers to be ideal Orthodoxy. Often, Rabbi Angel's writings are scholarly efforts to analyze and present various ideas and ideals of Judaism. There also is a regular hallmark of his writings to battle passionately and courageously for the very soul of Orthodoxy. Rabbi's Angel's writings are suffused with calm, thoughtful, well-researched wisdom, coupled with an urgent sense that these ideas must prevail or else our community is impoverished as a result.

Ideally, all Jews should be faithful to Torah and *halakhah*. However, even in a less-than-ideal world, we must view all Jews, regardless of level of observance, as a family. The inclusive communal model, which never fractured into various ideological movements, provides the best paradigm for promoting Jewish unity for a fragmented contemporary Jewish community. The Sephardic world, and many Ashkenazic communities, championed this inclusive model. Even within the halakhically observant community, the ideal is unity without conformity. There are many legitimate avenues to a Torah lifestyle.

We must try to win the hearts of all Jews to the Torah through persuasion and through exemplifying excellent religious and moral behavior, and never through authoritarianism or coercion. We should learn from everyone: the full range of rabbinic thought throughout the ages, folk wisdom, and the wisdom of the world. Judaism is a truth-seeking religion.

Rabbi Angel regularly appeals to a passage in the Jerusalem Talmud: The way of the Torah is a narrow path. To the right is fire and to the left is ice. Overzealousness leads to fiery extremism and fanaticism, whereas too much secularization or watering down of Jewish belief and observance leads to icy skepticism. The Torah way of life is balanced, harmonious and sensible. To be fulfilled properly, it must maintain its balance on the narrow path.

A confident faith is unafraid of questions and challenges. It is unafraid of diversity of opinion, and it is unafraid of ideas that force one to rethink one's own assumptions. The rabbinic axiom, "know how to answer the heretic" (Mishnah, *Avot* 2:14), requires a deep knowledge of what that heretic thinks, and a thoughtful understanding of why he or she rejects our traditions.

Judaism balances a particularistic aspect in which God has a singular relationship with the Jewish people through the Torah and *halakhah*; and a universalistic aspect which fosters genuine respect for all humanity. Jews should live in their divinely-given Torah path, while simultaneously embracing the Torah's ideal that God is everyone's God. The Torah's teaching, that all of humanity is created in the Image of God, should foster a genuine love and respect of humanity, and a desire to engage with the world, both its people and its wisdom. As Jews, we are responsible for all other Jews. As human beings, we are responsible for *yishuvo shel olam*—participating in the advancement of humanity.

Judaism is broad, and contemporary society needs its broadness to address the complex religious and communal realities of today. We also need to represent the profound sophistication and wisdom of Jewish tradition at its best to appeal to well-educated Jews.

There are two fundamental approaches to applying *halakhah* to real life. One approach begins with a study of the classical rabbinic texts, reaching a scholarly conclusion, and then applying that conclusion to the individual or community. The other approach begins with the human reality and then studies the classical rabbinic texts for principles to apply to that reality. Rabbi Angel strongly favors the latter approach. For example, when addressing the question of saying Psalms of Praise (Hallel) on Yom HaAtzmaut (Israel's Independence Day), we must begin by acknowledging the religious reality of the miracle of the State of Israel. Only then do we turn to the halakhic books.

Ideal rabbis must be scholars and teachers of Torah, but also must be involved with the community. There needs to be a symbiotic relationship between local rabbis who know the particular needs of their communities, and rabbinic decisors who are experts in halakhic texts. Community rabbis must have the humility to consult halakhic experts, and they also must take responsibility to make decisions armed with that expert knowledge for their local communities. The Torah gives guidance for every aspect of life, and rabbinic leadership should offer that guidance to the community. Orthodoxy can exert its greatest influence when its representatives are involved in all communal matters.

The greatest role models behind Rabbi Angel's religious worldview are Rambam in the medieval period; and Rabbis Benzion Uziel, Haim David Halevy, and Joseph Soloveitchik in the twentieth century. On the communal leadership level, Rabbi Angel also admires two of his predecessors who led Congregation Shearith Israel: Dr. Henry Pereira Mendes and Dr. David de Sola Pool. These exceptional rabbis embodied the ideas and ideals of Judaism at the intellectual, communal, and personal levels.

We do not need to reinvent Judaism or Orthodoxy. We must find its most compelling elements from within our classical sources and promote them. The best of Judaism has the power to attract and inspire many Jews, and they in turn can create the positive model society to inspire humanity.

◇◇◇

Within the contemporary Orthodox world, there are powerful threats to Rabbi Angel's comprehensive vision. There are significant and growing strains within Orthodoxy that are overly fundamentalist. They teach Tanakh and the Talmud at a hyper-literal level, and ignore science, reason, and even the diversity of sacred Jewish texts that present other opinions. Some promote superstition. Some promote isolationism from less observant Jews, non-Jews, and any ideas that are foreign to the specific narrow ideas they espouse. Some overemphasize the particularistic elements of Judaism while ignoring the universalistic elements.

When Judaism is presented as isolationist and anti-reason, it distorts Jewish teaching and creates a cult-like religious group that cares only about its idea of God and the members of its small circle. This approach also alienates many intelligent, educated Jews who are made to feel that tradition and intellectual honesty are at odds with one another. In fact, they are completely intertwined.

Rabbi Angel frequently criticizes the attempt in certain segments of the Orthodox community to stifle legitimate diversity of opinion. One dimension of this problem is the phenomenon of self-selected "gedolim" (great rabbinic sages), who maintain that they alone possess the truth of Torah and therefore all other opinions are invalid and irrelevant. The vitality of Judaism relies on debate and conversations. A healthy Judaism allows ideas to be debated, accepted, or rejected, but never stifled or ignored.

This problem also extends to the proper balance between local rabbis and halakhic scholars who spend their time in *yeshivot*. The insistence of many today that *halakhah* must derive from sacred texts first and then applied to real-life situations undermines the ideal symbiotic relationship between local rabbis and halakhic decisors. Suddenly, halakhic experts are required not only to share their knowledge with the community rabbis, but also to *decide* policy for individual communities. As noted above, Rabbi Angel insists that proper *halakhah* must begin with the human reality and then turn to the classical rabbinic texts. Community rabbis must consult halakhic experts for the range of halakhic opinion, and then take responsibility for making the proper decision for their communities.

Another harmful restriction of opinion in many Orthodox circles is the frequent suppression of Sephardic voices of the past 500 years, generally through ignorance—whether willful or not. This bizarre reality is disrespectful to the sacred customs of Sephardic communities and causes pain to Sephardic yeshiva students who often feel excluded from "Jewish" experience. However, the harm on the communal level is far greater. The plethora of complex issues facing the contemporary Jewish community, including conversion to Judaism, the tragic *agunah* problem (a woman who is trapped in a dead marriage because her husband refuses to grant a religious writ of divorce, a *get*), issues pertaining to the modern State of Israel, the role of women, family values, contemporary modesty, and so many other issues, must be addressed with the full rabbinic toolbox. By stifling dissent and diversity, by ignoring the views of many Sephardic rabbis, and by adopting very restrictive positions, the Jewish community suffers irreparable damage.

Although advocates of more extremist, isolationist, restrictive, superstitious, and fundamentalist forms of Judaism cause harm on the intellectual and communal level, there is another culprit behind the flaws of the Orthodox community. Too many rabbis and laypeople remain silent or even tacitly support the more extreme views. Those who understand the ideas and ideals of the Torah must courageously stand up and promote the ideal vision of Judaism. The community must play a vital role by supporting institutions that promote these ideals.

Rabbi Angel quotes Rabbi Benzion Uziel, who in 1919 reminded his rabbinic colleagues that humility is praiseworthy, but it must never lead to shying away from the needs of the hour. Inertia cloaked in false humility is an abdication of one's responsibility as a leader. By writing articles with titles such as "On Torah Education and Mis-Education," "Reclaiming Orthodox Judaism," and "Re-Imagining Orthodox Judaism," Rabbi Angel draws his battle lines and appeals to the broader community to recognize the importance of standing up for these ideal values.

In his essay, "Reclaiming Orthodox Judaism," Rabbi Angel offers a remarkable analysis of a celebrated talmudic passage, the story of Kamtza and Bar Kamtza (*Gittin* 55b-56a). After a misunderstanding over a party invitation, Bar Kamtza was furious with the rabbis present who had remained silent at his humiliation. To retaliate, Bar Kamtza accused the Jews of rebellion to the Roman Emperor, suggesting that they would reject his sacrificial offering. The Emperor sent an offering, but Bar Kamtza made a slight blemish on the animal that would technically render the sacrifice invalid. When the rabbis discovered the blemish, most maintained that they should sacrifice the animal anyway, so as not to offend the Emperor. One rabbi named Zechariah ben Avkulas objected, since the law prohibits such a sacrifice. The rabbis then suggested killing Bar Kamtza so he could not inform on them to the Roman authorities. Again, Rabbi Zechariah objected, since Bar Kamtza had not committed a capital crime. As a consequence, Bar Kamtza returned to the Emperor, who was enraged against the Jewish community and destroyed the Temple. The story ends with a condemnation of the hardline position of Rabbi Zechariah: "Rabbi Yohanan thereupon remarked: Through the scrupulousness of Rabbi Zechariah ben Avkulas our House has been destroyed, our Temple burnt and we ourselves exiled from our land."

Rabbi Angel agrees with Rabbi Yohanan, that the hardline stand of Rabbi Zechariah was a disaster. Rabbi Zechariah placed book knowledge ahead of an obvious reality, namely, the Jewish community would be in dire peril if the rabbis rejected the sacrifice from the Emperor and allowed Bar Kamtza to inform against them. Clearly, the needs of the hour required the position of the majority, to make an emergency ruling to allow the sacrifice so that they could maintain the good favor of the Roman government.

However, continues Rabbi Angel, Rabbi Zechariah is not the true villain of this narrative. The ultimate failure should be ascribed to the majority of rabbis. Why did they not overrule the hardline position of this one rabbi? Evidently, they did not want to seem less religious, less committed to the sacred texts of the Torah. They had to take a risk by applying *halakhah* to a dire reality. The cowardly majority allowed the forceful insistence of Rabbi Zechariah to win the day—and therefore are complicit in the destruction of the Second Temple.

Rabbi Angel's analysis thereby sets out two of his central messages. First, when hardline halakhic analysis follows book knowledge prior to evaluating a living reality, *halakhah* can be distorted and it may cause harm to the community. Second, and in many ways more importantly, those whose judgment is sound must courageously stand up against the hardline position. When the majority of reasonable voices remain silent, voices of extremism prevail and the entire Jewish community loses.

In his essay, "Re-Imagining Orthodox Judaism," Rabbi Angel writes that "If enough of us share these ideals; if enough of us are willing to work to promote these ideals; if we can impact on synagogues, schools, and yeshivot—then perhaps these ideals will actually be realized in our community." Rabbi Angel is right. The rest is up to us to support and build on this foundation.

www.ingramcontent.com/pod-product-compliance
Lightning Source LLC
Chambersburg PA
CBHW031836090426
42741CB00005B/263